Live your life

A GUIDE TO PERSONAL & BUSINESS SUCCESS...

by Laurence Winmill

The right of Laurence Winmill to be identified as the author of this work has been asserted by him in accordance with the Copyright, Designs and Patents Act, 1988

ISBN: 978-0-9574894-0-0

LLYFRAU CAMBRIA

Published in the United Kingdom in 2013 by
Cambria Books; Carmarthenshire, Wales, United Kingdom

About the author:

Laurence Winmill is thought to be one of the most *dynamic*, *radical* and *creative* motivational speakers currently working the international circuit. His hard-hitting messages focus on the explosive combinations of attitude, drive, desire, belief, raw emotion and hard work.

Laurence talks about real life experiences from his business career which spans over the last thirty years. He talks about entrepreneurship and risk and his desire to pursue new creative business opportunities. Development, sales, customer service, management and various personal business anecdotes are featured throughout his presentations.

His vast experience has been documented over the years into a catalogue of books which feature some of the subjects that are close to his heart and responsible for his success in the business world. They include:

> Customer Service Jokers & Kings

> The Secrets of Successful Selling

> How to get more sales by asking better questions

> Close more sales by improving your conversion ratio

> First Class Communication & Presentation Skills

> Customer Service – Jokers & Kings CD Audio

> Open your Sales Presentation with a Brilliant Introduction

> Attitude – A Self-Assessment Test

He's been involved in the creation of various businesses over the years including video franchising, commercial vehicles, direct marketing, advertising and publishing.

His management experience is extensive having progressed through junior, middle, and senior management in advertising and marketing, to director of sales with a leading medical equipment and pharmaceutical supplies company.

In 2005 Laurence founded Avagio Limited, a publishing company specialising in consumer and business magazines which were distributed regionally throughout the UK. Despite some very challenging times during the financial crisis of 2008 which saw the business close, the core brands themselves survived and are now owned by one of the UK's leading publishers: Northcliffe Media. (Local World since 2013)

Laurence's story relating to this period is moving and very emotional as he explains the highs and lows associated with running a million pound business and then losing it. Despite the heartache of losing everything as recently as 2009, his determination to bounce back, move forward and build it all over again is unprecedented.

This latest book is an education manual, a collection of stories and references. It quotes the works of others who have inspired the author; it features the opportunities and challenges of life and it encapsulates Laurence's views and anecdotes which have inspired him personally over the years.

It is packed full of recommendations and action points to get you moving, enjoy the moment and live your life to its full potential!

Enjoy the read!

Contents

01.

Read more books

Read more books

Educate yourself. Take responsibility for your own learning. You can bet your bottom dollar that there will be thousands of educational and self-help books available on your chosen subject. But first of all you must get into the habit of reading and start to enjoy the value that reading provides. If for example you want to become a better salesperson I know from personal experience that there are approximately four thousand books currently available, full of helpful tips and ideas on selling.

Unlimited Learning Trivia – Brain Facts:

⇨ You have 15 times more neurons in your head than there are people on the planet.

⇨ You have as many connections in your brain as there have been seconds since the dinosaurs walked the earth.

⇨ If each of your brain cells was as big as a pinhead your brain would measure five metres across.

⇨ Your brain has 100 billion neurons and an ant has only 10,000 – yet we can both form complex societies.

⇨ Your brain weighs about 1.3kg or just under 3lb – heavier than a bag of sugar.

Source: www.at-bristol.org.uk/explore/amazing.htm

Things to do:

⇨ Decide what subject you wish to learn about – be specific.

⇨ Visit your local book store and familiarise yourself with what is available.

⇨ Use the internet, search for various books, subjects and titles.

⇨ Ask other people in your field of interest for their recommendations on any good books they may have read or are currently reading.

⇨ Develop a passion for reading. Learn to enjoy reading and the value it provides. Your enthusiasm and desire to read will grow when you realise how much more knowledgeable you've become through your reading.

⇨ Set aside reading time every day.

⇨ Set some reading goals:

> Make a list of books that you will definitely read over the next year and then buy them.

> Start to build your own private library.

> Set targets for the books you want to read in a month and then break this down into weeks.

> If you read one book a week, that would be 52 in a year. Just think – in 8 years you would have read over 400 books. And don't forget – with new books being published every year, your learning potential is endless.

> If you read up to 3 books per week, very quickly you will become so knowledgeable on your chosen subject that you'll most certainly become an expert in your field. Once you become an expert you can then consider writing your own books!

02.

Listen to podcasts & audios

Get an iPod

Listen to podcasts and audio books

In the 21st century there are so many different ways to learn. There is no doubt in my mind that one of the best learning opportunities available is through podcasts and audio books. The benefit of audio learning is that you can learn while you are travelling. Most people spend hours in their cars travelling up and down motorways listening to music. There is nothing wrong with listening to music, but imagine if you spent two hours in your car every day and you spent at least half of that time, say one hour, listening to an educational audio book each day. Applying some simple maths, the figures speak for themselves:

Let's take out weekends (105 days) plus holidays (25 days) and we still have 235 days or 235 learning hours, based on one hour per day. This equates to 29.4 working/learning days assuming a college or work based learning day of 8 hours. In 2013 the average cost of seminar based training for a delegate is around £350 per day, which means that you would have to outlay £10,290 to pay for this quality of training in a classroom.

The cost-effective use of audio learning when compared to the above is a great investment in your education and a constructive use of your idle time. Of course if you use trains, planes, or even boats the same investment principles apply.

Things to do:

⇨ Find out what's available.

⇨ You can be certain that if it's in print form it will also be available to download or as an audio book.

⇨ The internet is a great way to source what is available with vast amounts of apps and downloads at your disposal.

⇨ Get the balance right between audio, download and printed books – decide in advance your preferences for reading and listening.

⇨ Invest in an iPod or portable CD player – you can use it on the train, on a plane, a boat, even in the gym!

⇨ Start to build an audio library. Like good music it never goes out of fashion.

As with printed books, if you start to invest in this type of learning you will very quickly become extremely knowledgeable in your field. This knowledge will help you become a professional in your chosen subject, setting you apart from your competitors and providing you with opportunities that otherwise would not exist.

03.

Attend seminars and conferences

Attend seminars and conferences

Go to seminars and conferences – as many as you can in any single year. These are live events and you will always pick up nuggets of information to use and practise in your own field or industry. You might not like or agree with every speaker or trainer you listen to, but you will always find something of value to put to good use.

In most cases the speakers and trainers you meet at conferences will be experts in their fields. Their style may be different to yours but in nearly every instance they will have 'been there and worn the T-shirt'.

They would have experienced the highs and lows, failure and success; they will be able to speak with conviction and experience on their subject and because of that, they offer an invaluable learning experience and another great investment in your own personal development.

Trivia Fact – Einstein's brain was smaller than average because, he had a smaller than average physique. His superior intelligence came from the number of connections he made between his brain cells. Every time you learn something new you are making a new connection between two brain cells.
Source: www.at-bristol.org.uk/education/nesta/links.htm

Things to do:

⇨ Build a schedule of events for the year and decide which conferences and seminars you want to attend.

⇨ Be specific in your choice and prioritise those events you believe will add value to your learning experience.

⇨ Register with associations, chambers and trade bodies linked to your industry and research what events are available throughout the year.

⇨ When attending these events listen, learn and network at every opportunity.

⇨ Take plenty of business cards with you and be prepared to collect as many business cards in return.

⇨ Make a point of approaching the speakers or trainers during a break or at the end of the conference to ask them questions specific to your learning needs.

⇨ Pay to go to at least three events a year out of your own pocket. These events will probably be the best you attend. Because you have paid, you will undoubtedly value them more and you will have shown your commitment to investing seriously in your own personal development.

04.

Invest 4% of your gross income into your own personal development

Invest 4% of your gross income in your own personal development

In order to fund your learning and education, re-invest a minimum of 4% of every penny you earn back into a personal development fund. Books, audio learning, seminars, training and conferences all cost money, but it's money well spent because it's investing in your development and your future. It's as important as any pension scheme because this investment will dictate your earning potential for the rest of your working life. The greater your knowledge and understanding on a subject, the more likely you are to be successful in whatever career you decide to follow.

Success stems from confidence. People become confident practising their skills when they feel comfortable in their own ability to perform. Any athlete who wants to perform competitively follows a similar path:

An athlete invests in a coach to help them perfect technique. The coach understands through knowledge, learning and experience the benefits associated with good technique. This technique is taught by the coach and then practised repeatedly by the athlete until they become familiar and comfortable with its function and the benefit it provides. Eventually the winning combination of belief, desire, technique and natural ability results in gold medals and championship titles.

Minimum investment guide:

> Annual salary – £10,000 – investment = £400

> Annual salary – £20,000 – investment = £800

> Annual salary – £25,000 – investment = £1000

> Annual salary – £50,000 – investment = £2000

> Annual salary – £100,000 – investment = £4000

Things to do:

⇨ Make a commitment to invest in you.

⇨ Ask yourself how much are you worth and how much money you would like to earn.

⇨ Decide how valuable an asset you currently are, and set yourself a target for where you would like to be in terms of your employment value:

> 6 months from now

> 1 year from now

> 18 months from now

> 2 years from now

> 5 years from now

⇨ Set yourself **SMART** Goals to achieve your desires:

> SPECIFIC

> MEASURABLE

> ACHIEVABLE

> REALISTIC

> TIMESCALE/TARGETED

Once you commit to investing in you, you send a signal to yourself and everyone around you that you take yourself seriously, that you are focused on your goals and, more importantly, you are absolutely serious about developing into the person you truly want to be.

05.

Seek a well balanced life:

a   Family
b   Professional
c   Social
d   Spiritual
e   Educational

Seek a well balanced life

Happy people are normally very productive people and generally-speaking, people enjoy associating with happy, productive and, of course, successful individuals.

The key to happiness is to have a balance in your life which allows you to share your time equally amongst the people and things which are important to you: work, family, leisure, education and spiritual beliefs.

It's great to have ambitions and goals but it's also important to appreciate the present and what you already have. Enjoy every moment of every day, learn to smile again and start to appreciate what you have close by which everyone tends to take for granted from time to time.

Potential happiness is sometimes so close that we don't recognise it for what it is. The following story is a wonderful example which I found some years ago, sent to me by Peter Thomson one of the UK's leading strategists on business and personal growth and highlights the value tied to the simple things in life. It helps you re-evaluate what's important to you!

The Mexican Boatman

An American investment banker was at the pier of a small coastal Mexican village when a small boat with just one fisherman docked. Inside the small boat were several large yellow-fin tuna. The American complimented the Mexican on the quality of his fish and asked how long it took to catch them.

The Mexican replied, "Only a little while."

The American then asked why didn't he stay out longer and catch more fish. The Mexican said he had enough to support his family's immediate needs.

The American then asked, "But what do you do with the rest of your time?"

The Mexican fisherman said, "I sleep late, fish a little, play with my children, take a siesta with my wife, Maria, stroll into the village each evening where I sip wine and play guitar with my amigos. I have a full and busy life."

The American scoffed, "I am a Harvard MBA and could help you. You should spend more time fishing and with the proceeds buy a bigger boat. With the proceeds from the bigger boat you could buy several boats, eventually you would have a fleet of fishing boats.

Instead of selling your catch to a middleman you would sell directly to the processor, eventually opening your own cannery.

You would control the product, processing and distribution.

You would need to leave this small coastal fishing village and move to Mexico City, then LA and eventually NYC where you will run your expanding enterprise."

The Mexican fisherman asked, "But how long will this all take?"

To which the American replied, "Fifteen to twenty years."

"But what then?"

The American laughed and said that's the best part. "When the time is right you would announce an IPO (Initial Purchase Offer) and sell your company stock to the public and become very rich. You would make millions."

"Millions. Then what?"

The American said, "Then you would retire. Move to a small coastal fishing village where you would sleep late, fish a little, play with your kids, take a siesta with your wife, Maria, stroll to the village in the evenings where you could sip wine and play your guitar with your amigos."

The above tale is a classic which I never get sick of reading. Very often in today's 'Now' and the 'Must Have' society, we get caught up in life's merry-go-round and end up missing out what should be important to us: family, children, friendships and relaxation time. The sixty-four thousand dollar question is, "Why do we allow this to happen?"

Lately I have taken the step to re-evaluate my life. I believe that life is not for thinking endlessly about what you don't have, but to enjoy and appreciate what you already have!

Things to do:

➪ Love your work and your job satisfaction will ensure that you produce fantastic results.

➪ If you hate your job – change it. You're not doing yourself or your employer any favours by hanging on for the regular monthly wage slip. Life is too short to be unhappy day after day.

➪ Re-evaluate what is important to you and then focus on making it happen.

➪ Set goals in your personal life as well as your business life.

➪ Travel whenever you can and experience the different cultures and wonders of the world.

➪ Learn to laugh again. Children laugh on average 108 times a day. A typical adult laughs only 8.

➪ Be happy in your relationships and at home.

➪ Read a bedtime story to your kids.

➪ Exercise regularly and get back in touch with nature. Go for walks in the countryside or to the seaside. Watch the stars at night. Pick a day and watch the sun rise and then pick a night and watch the sun set.

➪ Be at peace with yourself.

➪ Invest in lifelong learning and enjoy life.

06.
Right behaviour– right results

Right behaviour – right results

How do you bridge the gap between average performance and great performance?

Can you educate yourself to become an expert in your field? Will a degree or another academic or professional qualification guarantee better job prospects? Will being coached by a mentor or professional person improve your overall success rates?

The simple answer to those three questions is yes. You can read, research and learn from a thousand and one different sources; with so many courses available these days, you can get a qualification in almost anything. There are always benefits to be gained from speaking and listening to those with experience and expertise such as professional coaches. True success, though, comes back to the question posed in the opening sentence: how do you bridge the gap between average performance and great performance?

Everyone will have an opinion on this but I firmly believe that the very best people in any organization are those with the ability to communicate and build rapport with others. Core communication skills are always associated with certain human characteristics and it is excelling in these areas which really separate the great from the good.

Organizations all over the world are made up of good people but it's the great people who generate the great results. Pareto's 80:20 Rule certainly applies in business as any manager or director can confirm: 80% of the business invariably comes from 20% of the team.

So why are these special people so few and far between? I believe the answer is very simple – understand and possess certain characteristics and you will fall into the top 10% in any team in any environment. With further education and coaching you will become more polished and professional in whatever you do.

Like many young people learning their trade in sporting academies all over the world, the same principle applies to almost anything you choose to do. Only a very small percentage will realise their full potential and move into the Premier League, able to compete with the very best in the world.

Having practised and researched people's performance levels for over thirty years I have compiled a list of the core human characteristics displayed by the best in their chosen field. Put simply: the characteristics that separate the great from the good.

Things to do:

⇨ **Develop real belief.** Successful people believe in themselves. They have strong values and their conviction in what they do is obvious to all those who come into contact with them.

⇨ **Become enthusiastic about everything you do.** This is an outer reflection of your inner belief. Enthusiasm is infectious and raises the positive connections between people. Rapport is established and trust begins to develop.

⇨ **Demonstrate true commitment/dedication.** Committed people are successful people. You may remember the popular 1970's TV programme, *The Record Breakers*. It featured individuals who broke records and became recognised as the best in their field. The presenter, the late Roy Castle, would always end the programme by singing:

"Remember, if you want to be the best, if you want to beat the rest, dedication is what you need…"

⇨ **Make a great first impression – be aware of your voice/tone/ smile/presentation.** All that you've heard about first impressions being important, is true. You will probably make up your mind about someone during the first thirty seconds of your meeting or conversation and if you don't like what you hear or see then you are highly unlikely to do business with them. So make sure your first impression is the best you can make it. Be positive, stay focused, make eye contact, smile and when you speak, be confident, clear, concise and to the point

⇨ **Be on fire with desire / ego drive.** People with desire are winners. Powerful desires allow people to set realistic goals and they become accustomed to achieving goals and success on a regular basis. Nothing will stand in their way as the drive of their ego forces them through barriers and obstacles to achieve successes that most people simply dream about.

⇨ **Demonstrate great empathy** – the ability to understand, to tune into someone's way of thinking. If you put yourself in the shoes of another person and understand what it is they are feeling, then you will develop great rapport and trust with them.

⇨ **Show loyalty** – a powerful value. Being recognised as a person with integrity is another important quality helping to build trust in others. People do business with people they like and trust.

⇨ **Become a great listener.** The majority of people talk, very few listen! The best conversationalists are those who ask questions and listen to the answers. By listening carefully you demonstrate real interest in the other person which allows you to identify any needs they might have. If you are in business this is an essential part of the customer service process.

⇨ **Develop the skill of persuasion** – an important characteristic during any negotiation stage. Throughout life we are constantly selling ourselves to others and the ability to persuade people to believe in you, whether it is in business or for pleasure, will determine how successful you are.

"If you can't explain it simply, you don't understand it well enough"
Albert Einstein, German Physicist (1879-1955)

⇨ **Demonstrate and exhibit a positive attitude.** This tenth characteristic pulls together the attributes of the nine above — and delivers more. It is without doubt the key characteristic for success in all walks of life. It separates the winners from the losers. It is the difference of being liked or disliked. It is the one single factor that sees some people achieving their goals and ambitions while others falter. It is a characteristic that stands out in the very best politicians, leaders, sports people, and winners across the globe.

"There is little difference in people, but that little difference makes a big difference. The little difference is attitude. The big difference is whether it is positive or negative."
W. Clement Stone

07.

Believe in
what you do

Believe in what you do

If you believe, then anything is possible. The opposite is also true – if you don't believe then everything you seek or desire becomes impossible. Everyone comes into this world with the opportunity to do something with his or her life. Being born into money does not guarantee happiness or success but having a great belief in your own ambitions will certainly drive you towards your goals irrespective of your circumstances.

It is your desire, and not your ability, that determines success and if you truly believe in your own capabilities then anything becomes possible.

Belief is an inner quality. When you become passionate about your beliefs, this transforms into enthusiasm, which is an outer reflection of your inner self. When you are enthusiastic about something your motivation and commitment levels become automatic – nothing will stand in your way.

The great benefit of truly believing in yourself and your ambitions is that other people will see this belief, will take you seriously and they in turn will truly believe in you as a person.

Things to do:

⇨ Make a list of all your successes to date. Build a success library – it will boost your confidence and will help you remember the good times when things aren't going so well.

⇨ Banish negative thoughts and replace them with thoughts of you succeeding in your chosen goal.

⇨ Create pictures in your mind of you achieving real success. Imagine yourself achieving your goals and desires. These powerful images will drive you forward to eventual success.

⇨ Start to believe in your own ability to succeed. If you believe in you then people around you will believe in you too.

⇨ Set realistic goals and focus on making progress to realize them.

⇨ Remember that everyone has to work hard to achieve their ambitions and most people fail because they give up too easily. Keep going when the going gets tough.

⇨ Don't be put off by setbacks. Real winners are the people who never, ever give up:

Roger Bannister was told the four minute mile was impossible – yet he became the first person to break the four minute mark!

Michael Jordan was dropped from his school basketball team – yet he went on to become the best player that ever lived!

Both Henry Ford and Walt Disney experienced bankruptcy early in their careers – but they never gave up their dreams!

Bob Dylan was booed off stage at a high school talent show but he still went on to become a musical legend!

08.

Inspire others

Inspire others

Life is about balance and that means giving and providing as well as taking. We all enjoy receiving gifts and surprises – it creates pleasure and brings a smile to our face. But what can beat the sensational feeling of seeing the pleasure your gift has brought to someone else. That is why there is always more value and greater reward in giving rather than receiving.

Giving, of course, doesn't have to be in a monetary or material sense because the most valuable things in life are still free. Providing love, faith and time to people who are important in your life is far more rewarding. Very often all that is required is a hug or a smile or some reassuring words to remind them how important and valuable they really are.

Of course, people also need role models and mentors – individuals to look up to – who can provide the inspiration they need to achieve their own goals and ambitions. True champions in any field always give back and contribute to tomorrow's champions by offering advice, support, coaching and the sharing of their experiences.

Things to do:

⇨ Give those closest to you the most precious things of all – your love and your time.

⇨ Operate with total integrity and create a set of strong values that reflect your beliefs.

⇨ Get active in your community and make a real contribution.

⇨ Become a mentor in your chosen field and inspire others by passing on your experiences. Set new challenges and demonstrate your continued appetite for success to others.

We all need inspiration from time to time and there is nothing more inspiring than seeing humble people overcoming personal challenges to achieve success. Ask others about their stories, encourage them to move forward and inspire them by sharing your own journey to success.

09.

Empathy - show
real appreciation
of other people's
circumstances

Empathy

Show real appreciation of other people's circumstances

Empathy is a very powerful human characteristic and should not be mistaken for sympathy. Feeling sorry for someone is not going to help the other person move forward from any given circumstance. Empathy enables you to connect with another person; it allows you to have a real understanding of how they are feeling and to appreciate without passing judgement.

This is a rare quality in business but by simply having empathy you immediately have an advantage over your competitors. Being able to see things from their point of view allows you to objectively assess your own reactions given the same set of circumstances.

People warm to those who are empathetic, they know they are being listened to and taken seriously. Because of this emotional connection, trust develops and so too does the opportunity to develop the business relationship.

Sometimes people find it difficult to understand the real meaning of empathy but a simple analogy would be to compare the use of a missile aimed towards a target:

During the Second World War, London was the subject of severe carpet-bombing by the Luftwaffe, famously depicted in the film "Battle of Britain". British artillery units were positioned in key strategic sites to try to defend the capital by shooting German aircraft out of the sky. Despite winning the battle, the collateral damage and the cost of human life in London was immense because many of the missiles aimed at the enemy aircraft simply missed their target.

If the aircraft felt threatened at any time they took evasive action to avoid being shot down and, because the shell or missile was unable to change course, it missed its target.

Today, however, technology has moved on and such an encounter in the 21st century would involve surface to air missiles which once fired, homes in on its target, using the heat generated by the target's engine. The heat-seeking missile continues to hunt its target until it makes a connection despite any evasive action attempted by the target.

It's a little dramatic but a great way to understand how a person with empathy might operate. For example, a sales person with empathy would not be thrown off-course by any objections that arose. As a result, they would connect with the customer, understand their needs and gather a full appreciation of the customer's business. Invariably, once the needs are identified, the sales person is able to match the needs with the products and services they are selling and go on to close the sale.

Things to do:

⇨ Become a better listener. Look at the other person when they are speaking and acknowledge what is being said.

⇨ Question politely anything that you don't fully understand.

⇨ Use consistent body language such as positive gestures, an open stance and an upright posture. Be friendly and make eye contact.

⇨ Chose your words carefully and use vocabulary that demonstrates to people that you are listening and you are taking them seriously.

⇨ Try to see the good and not the bad in others.

⇨ Think before you respond to another person by asking yourself "How would I be feeling if I were that person and what response would I ideally like to hear?" You might not be able to tell them exactly what they want to hear but having a sincere appreciation of their feelings, will shine through.

10.
Smile

Smile

It's one of the most positive and powerful human gestures that exists. It connects one person to another and displays warmth and affection. It helps build bridges, breaks down barriers and sends signals of well-being and sincerity. We should never underestimate the power and value of a smile.

I read recently that the average child laughs 108 times a day, but then the child grows up and becomes an adult. The fun disappears from life which is reflected in the number of times an adult laughs a day – a paltry 8 times in comparison! Why does the ability to laugh decline so dramatically?

Happy people are productive people.

The transmission of happiness begins with a smile. Smiling and laughing release powerful chemicals in the brain called endorphins. Endorphins have a positive effect on the way we feel about ourselves and towards others. The more we smile, the more we laugh and the more we laugh, the happier we are as people.

Happy people are productive people.

People like to be associated with happy, productive and ultimately successful people. Customers like to be greeted by happy, friendly staff. Employees enjoy working for happy employers and employers enjoy employing happy, friendly staff.

Life's best relationships are forged when happy, friendly people come together. The power of the smile is truly unlimited.

Things to do:

⇨ Learn to smile again. Practice in the mirror – you'll be amazed what you see!

⇨ Seek happiness with a well balanced life – remember the Mexican fisherman.

⇨ Learn to love your work.

⇨ Learn to love the present. Don't dwell on the past and plan – but don't worry about – the future.

⇨ Look for the good in people and in every situation.

⇨ Lighten up, life's too short.

⇨ Laugh and enjoy the simple things in life.

⇨ Greet everyone you meet with a genuine, friendly smile.

⇨ When problems occur, accept them as part of life. Smile, deal with them and move on.

⇨ Make a habit of making people happy every day of your life.

⇨ Smiling exercises your facial muscles and keeps you looking good!

⇨ Read books, watch videos, or listen to audio books that make you smile.

Life is too short to be miserable, so learn to smile, force yourself to lighten up and smile about things that in the past may have made you mad. Smiling is infectious. If your smile is genuine and sincere then the chances are that others around you will contract the virus and they will start smiling too. The whole smiling experience is totally positive and the benefits will have a major impact on your life because of the sparkling, memorable impressions that you'll make on the lives of others.

11.

Listen

Listen

Great conversationalists are renowned for their ability to listen to what the other person is saying. They acknowledge the other person's conversation through consistent eye contact and use of body language such as nodding their head in agreement or raising a hand to question a particular point. The conversation deepens through the use of skilful questioning to probe the speaker's answers and explanations encouraging further elaboration of the key points.

The master conversationalist spends 80% of their time listening and 20% questioning and probing the points raised during the course of the conversation.

Active listening improves our credibility and our esteem amongst others. We become respected as people who genuinely take an interest in what others have to say, and we learn a lot more than those who choose to talk relentlessly about themselves.

How many times have you been to a party where you are introduced to someone only to forget their name minutes later?

The initial embarrassment only worsens when you find yourself in the situation of having to introduce your new acquaintance to someone else, yet you can't remember their name! A situation which could have been avoided if you hadn't been so focused on what you wanted to say and had paid attention to the conversation around you.

This is very common behaviour in both business and leisure where people are too concerned with the sound of their own voice. They would gain more influence and respect if they learned to give others opportunities to speak and listened constructively.

Things to do:

⇨ Discipline yourself to listen to others, concentrate on people's names and faces. People appreciate being remembered and acknowledged when you address them by name.

⇨ Practise listening by memorising names and events through visualisation. Associate names with memorable events. For example, if someone introduces you to Harry, visualise this particular Harry as Harry Potter whizzing around on a broomstick!

⇨ Look at the other person when they are talking to you, maintain eye contact and show interest by nodding and questioning key points.

⇨ Pay compliments when compliments are due during the course of the conversation.

⇨ Ask people's opinions. People love giving opinions and it makes them feel valued and important.

⇨ Take people seriously. If you are listening you're taking them seriously.

⇨ Ask questions, listen carefully to the answers and you will build meaningful conversations that will help you find out what makes people tick, their motivations and needs. Remember you have two ears and one mouth. You should always be able to listen twice as hard as you speak!

12.

Be happy

Be happy!

I make no apologies for repeating some of the things we covered earlier. We talked about seeking well-balanced lives and the benefits that the simple smile can contribute to people's overall happiness. But ultimately those references are part of a process, a process that helps us to be genuinely happy and content as individuals. Life is simply too short to be anything other than happy, but happiness is a state of mind: it's how you feel about you and your current situation.

You have no control over the past and although you can set plans and goals which drive positive behaviour, you simply cannot predict what the future will bring – so learn to enjoy the moment.

Enjoy the rain and the wind as much as you enjoy the sunshine and you'll start to appreciate all that's good around you. The things you once perceived as grey and dreary you will begin to see in a completely different light. When you're stuck in a traffic jam or things aren't going your way, view it as another one of life's situations. Look for the opportunity in the adversity – listen to an audio book in a traffic jam instead of becoming angry about a situation over which you have no control. Accept it and move on.

There is no benefit in holding grudges or allowing the past to make you miserable – this is negative energy which will fester inside you like a cancer causing you distress and unhappiness. It is far better to forgive, forget and move on, learning from the experience rather than allowing it to eat into your present and future happiness.

Look for the good in everyone and everything. Seek the peace of mind that will allow you to sleep at night and make you happy with yourself and all of those around you.

Things to do:

⇨ Don't allow the past to disrupt your present and future happiness.

⇨ Accept problems as a part of life. Learn, smile and move on.

⇨ Learn to love your life. If things are happening that are genuinely making you unhappy, change them.

⇨ Be content with you and the person you are. If you don't like what you see in the mirror – physically or emotionally – change things. You are in control of you.

⇨ Appreciate your environment. There's no point moaning about the weather – you can't control it. Learn to enjoy it. Take a walk in the rain – you get wet, big deal, you'll soon dry out and you might enjoy the experience!

⇨ Start to see yourself in a positive light. Think happy thoughts and visualise yourself laughing and enjoying life. The power of visualisation is huge – when you start to see it, you start to believe and when you believe, chances are it will happen.

⇨ And finally – some wise words from an earlier chapter:

Happy people are productive people.

The transmission of happiness begins with a smile. Smiling and laughing release powerful chemicals in the brain called endorphins. Endorphins have a positive effect on the way we feel about ourselves and towards others. The more we smile, the more we laugh and the more we laugh, the happier we are.

People like to be associated with happy, productive and ultimately successful people. Customers like to be greeted by happy, friendly staff. Employees enjoy working for happy employers and employers enjoy employing happy, friendly staff.

Life's best relationships are forged when happy, friendly people come together. The power of the smile is truly unlimited.

13.

Do not
fear failure

Do not fear failure

Many people fail before they start. Why? The answer is simple: they fear failure!

We are back to visualisation. If a sportsman was preparing for a major race and visualised himself losing then I guarantee he would lose.

There is no point lining up for the race if your state of mind tells you that you are about to fail. The same applies in business, relationships, performing in front of an audience or simply arranging a date with someone you fancy.

Anticipate failure and your mental state of mind will guarantee that you fail!

On the other hand, if you visualise success, then, although success is never guaranteed, you will certainly have the satisfaction of performing to your potential – and that is real success.

If you do perform to your potential and still fail, then so what? Keep trying until you succeed but never, ever give up. It's those who give up that are the real victims of failure. If you keep trying, failure never wins, you win. You become invincible. Your motivation will be so high that nothing will be impossible and although you may have to try and try again, you will finally achieve your goals. The fact that you no longer fear failure brings its own guaranteed success.

Remember these examples from chapter 7. These guys never gave up. They never allowed failure to deter them from achieving their ultimate goals:

Roger Bannister was told the four minute mile was impossible – yet he became the first person to break the four minute mark!

Michael Jordan was dropped from his school basketball team – yet he went onto become the best player that ever lived!

Both Henry Ford and Walt Disney experienced bankruptcy early in their careers – but they never gave up their dreams!

Bob Dylan was booed off stage at a high school talent show, but he still went on to become a musical legend!

Here is a great story supplied by Peter Thomson TGI Mondays about one of the finest inventors in history – Thomas Edison – and his many attempts to create an electric light:

Edison had tried out three thousand different theories while experimenting on the electric light and his quote is this:

"I was never discouraged – but I cannot say the same for other people who were working with me"

Thomas Edison didn't know the meaning of failure and certainly wasn't going to allow three thousand of them to stand between him and his ambition to create the electric light.

His breakthrough finally arrived when he decided to use a vacuum inside the bulb so that the filament didn't burn out so quickly. The problem was finding the right filament. He and his assistants tried every imaginable substance: barium, rhodium, ruthenium, titanium, platinum, zirconium, bamboo, cotton. Everything and anything. Week in, week out – for over a year at Edison's laboratory at Menlo Park in Middlesex County, New Jersey.

Finally, after working through the night, on the morning of the 22 October 1879 at just 32 years old, Edison and his team managed to seal a carbonised thread of cotton into a pear-shaped bulb and pump out the air.

Edison turned on the current and the lamp glowed like sunshine in the dusk of early autumn. They waited for it to burn out quickly as had happened previously. However the bulb remained alight. They waited. Hours passed, meal times came and went. All the workers at Menlo Park came and stared. Edison didn't go home to sleep that night or the next. The bulb burned for forty-five hours non-stop. Yes, forty-five hours. They had cracked the problem and invented the electric light bulb.

There is an old saying which is often banded around sales environments: "Persistence overcomes resistance". In Edison's case this was certainly true. Most people give up after one attempt, never mind three thousand!

There is nothing wrong with failing because failing allows us to learn. What is wrong is allowing failure to deter you from ever trying again.

Things to do:

⇨ Visualise yourself succeeding rather than failing.

⇨ If at first you don't succeed, re-focus and try again. Remember Edison – never give up!

⇨ Start to believe in you. Strong beliefs will motivate you towards obtaining your goals.

⇨ The risk of failure can be reduced through preparation, planning and research, but ultimately, if you don't try you won't turn your plans and dreams into reality.

⇨ Talk to people who have overcome failure to achieve their dreams. Let them inspire you to do the same.

⇨ Read books about real-life winners and achievers.

⇨ Start to record your successes.

⇨ Start to think positively about everything you do. Banish those negative demons that will prevent you from trying.

⇨ A dream is just a goal that can come true if you focus on making it become a reality.

⇨ If you fail at something, learn from your mistakes so the next time you won't fail at that same stage. Sooner or later by eliminating everything that doesn't work, you will find the formula for success.

Finally if you are sincere about achieving and being successful in your own right, you will achieve. Your drive and focus will allow you to deal with whatever failures and challenges occur along your journey as you pursue your dreams.

Remember the Wizard of Oz. There were many challenges along the yellow brick road but eventually the lion, the tin man, the scarecrow and Dorothy herself all fulfilled their dreams. Each overcame their personal challenges and continued along the road, irrespective of the obvious dangers. They were focused and had faith that they would eventually, despite the risks, overcome their fears and realise their dreams.

Go follow your yellow brick road.

14.

Take pride in your presentation and appearance

Take pride in your presentation and appearance

Presentation and first impressions are everything when you're meeting and dealing with people. As our lives are dominated by how people influence us and how we influence others, you will appreciate how important it is to get it right first time, every time.

It is a proven fact that people have formed an opinion of you during the first ten seconds of your meeting, and most will have made up their minds completely within the next thirty. Perhaps you are beginning to appreciate the statement:

"You only have one opportunity to make a first impression".

Your presentation is not only about how you look, it's the whole package and it starts with how you feel about yourself. If you don't feel pride in who you are, how you look and what you do, then how can you expect other people to hold a different view?

It doesn't matter what social background you come from, or how well educated you are, what is important in presentation is how you feel about ***you.*** You are a person just like the billions of other people on this planet and you have the same right to be here as anyone else – irrespective of your ethnic background, social class or religious beliefs.

When you start to love who you are, you will see life in a completely different light. Accept and learn to love your body and the way you approach life. Everyone knows the difference between good and bad and although you might get away with kidding everyone from time to time, you won't fool the person who faces you in the mirror each morning and at the end of every day.

Allow your better judgement to guide you in the right direction. Do the right things, feel good about yourself and your self-esteem will go from strength to strength.

When this happens, what you're wearing becomes irrelevant because the power of your smile and the presence of the **Real You** will create an impression that will make a huge impact on everyone you meet.

Things to do:

⇨ If you cannot convince yourself to love and like what you see, then you must take action to change it. If you think you are too fat, eat less and start an exercise programme. Join a gym and seek proper advice on diet and exercise.

⇨ If you think you are too thin, eat more (sensibly) and tone your body accordingly.

⇨ If you don't like your hair, change the colour, or maybe the style. Seek advice from a hair consultant at a salon of your choice.

⇨ If you don't like your wardrobe and the clothes you wear, set about slowly replacing them with those that make you feel good about yourself.

⇨ If your friends are getting you down through negative chatter and behaviour, change them. Seek the company of those who help you feel more positive about yourself and life.

⇨ Start to believe in you. Trust the person who is looking back in the mirror – make sure it's the person you want to see.

⇨ Put your shoulders back, hold your head up high and walk the talk. There's a whole new world out there just waiting to meet you.

⇨ Be sensible. You are what you eat and what you wear! Be comfortable with your external appearance professionally and socially. If you feel comfortable with the outside you'll feel a million dollars on the inside.

⇨ Set the world alight with a beaming, positive smile which, says you are sincere, genuine and you'll be somebody that everyone else will want to meet.

The author Emmet Fox makes a great point called "Tail Wags the Dog" and it's from his book "*Make Your Life Worthwhile*". In part it reads, "Truth is that your outer conditions – your environment – are the expression of your mentality, and nothing more. They are not cause; they are effect. They do not come first; they follow after...You do not have faith because things are going well. They are going well because you have faith. You are not depressed because trouble has come to you, but trouble has come because your realization of the Truth had first fallen off. Man is not limited by his environment. He creates his environment by his beliefs and feelings. To suppose otherwise is like thinking that the tail can wag the dog."

Finally, remember:
"First Impression – Fantastic Impression – Every time".
People flock towards positive, happy, sociable people and it all begins during those initial but critical thirty seconds. Believe in you, respect and love you. By liking the person you are, you will create a kind of magical, magnetic force which will attract people wherever you go.

15.

Learn to love

Learn to love

What is love? There are so many definitions and interpretations that it is sometimes easy to forget what it really means. I found the following definition in a dictionary and I think it's pretty close to what love should really mean to us all:

Love – *"The benevolence, kindness or brotherhood that human beings should rightfully feel towards others"*.

Love in its truest sense is surely one of the most powerful emotions that exist amongst mankind. Money can't buy it and people can't come between it. You can't see or touch it, but it exists in body and soul with energy so great that it survives famine, war and even death. It bonds us closely to those who matter most to us and allows us to forgive those who have plotted against us.

There is no negative in love. It is a positive emotion, a supercharged energy and if we could bottle and market its essence, its value would be priceless.

The most precious things in life really are free and love typifies that statement. If it's free and it is as powerful as we say, then why don't we see more of it? Why do we not find time for those who matter? Why do we lose touch with important friends? Why do we lose sight of our values and what we're about? Why is there never enough time in a day to put the important things first?

Unfortunately in the 21st century, time is premium and premium is money and while this is important, it can't buy you love.

A poem hangs on the wall in Mother Theresa's orphanage in India. It is a wonderful reminder of the example set by this humble saint, and which we should try follow in our crazy, fast-moving lives. I can't think of anything more appropriate to put in this "Things to do" section:

Things to do:

⇨ People are illogical, unreasonable and self-centred (including me). Love them anyway.

⇨ If you do well, people will accuse you of selfish, ulterior motives. Do good anyway.

⇨ If you are successful, you win false friends and true enemies. Succeed anyway.

⇨ The good you do today will be forgotten tomorrow. Do good anyway.

⇨ Honesty and frankness make you vulnerable. Be honest and frank anyway.

⇨ The biggest people with the biggest ideas can be shot down by the littlest people with the littlest ideas. Think big anyway.

⇨ People favour underdogs, but follow only top dogs. Fight for a few underdogs anyway.

⇨ What you spend years building may be destroyed overnight. Build anyway.

⇨ People really need help, but may attack you if you do help them. Help them anyway.

⇨ Give the world the best you have and you will get kicked in the teeth. Give the best you have anyway.

The above contains some wonderful advice from a very humble place, where love is available in abundance.

Start today by giving more love. Don't forget the more you invest the more you'll get back. It will be the biggest and most worthwhile investment of your entire life. The following list is not given in order of importance, as love should be equal.

> Love yourself
> Love your children
> Love your family
> Love your enemy
> Love your environment
> Love your life
> Love the God of your religion

> Love your partner
> Love your parents
> Love your friends
> Love your neighbour
> Love your work
> Love your world

16.

Set new challenges & goals

a. Professional
b. Spiritual
c. Social
d. Family
e. Educational

Set new challenges and goals

This chapter is dedicated to people and personal achievement. What I write will reflect the great human spirit and while paying tribute to success, the real aim is to inspire you to achieve your goals in your life.

Anything is possible if you want it badly enough, so sit back, enjoy the stories and use the inspiration to achieve your personal dreams and ambitions.

Successful superstars are no different from you and I; they simply don't know the meaning of failure – they never give up!

As a British man, I am tremendously inspired and proud when our sporting representatives become international legends as a result of their spectacular achievements on the world stage.

One Sunday night in December 2004 I tuned in to the BBC's Sports Personality of the year, which was honouring the great sporting achievements by our sports men and women throughout 2004.

There were many tributes made during the course of the evening, but four stood out above everything else and reminded me of the sacrifice, grit, courage, belief and ultimate desire that push these people through adversity and pain until their ultimate dream is achieved.

The Team of the Year award went to the British coxless four rowing crew, led by Matthew Pinsent who won the Olympic gold medal in Athens. I read an article in a national newspaper a couple of days after their victory which brings home how tough the race was and the fine margin of victory that separates winners from losers:

"There comes a point when the word pain alone does not describe it. When the toll, physical and emotional, is very nearly too much to bear; when the mental ruin, the enormity of the moment, the intense suffering in every muscle and fibre of the body becomes bewildering, almost overwhelming.

Matthew Pinsent and his crew reached that point and then dug deeper for 10 strokes more.

In those moments the boat moved ahead of the Canadian boat. Not by much, but by enough (30cms approx). Only eight one hundredths of a second separated the teams as they crossed the line, a margin so small neither group could be sure it had won and both prepared for the worst.

When it was over Pinsent – by nature an unemotional giant of a man – began to sob.

This had been some journey. Whatever the future holds for Pinsent, the force of this experience is unlikely to be surpassed."

The British public acknowledged this fantastic effort by voting this world conquering team as their "Team of the Year". Matthew Pinsent is a giant of a man who during his rowing career collected four Olympic gold medals. His place in sporting history is secured.

The second award I'd like to make reference to is the BBC Lifetime Achievement award, which honours true sporting legends who have become national and international icons as a result of their contributions to sport and society in general.

The winner was a man who dominated English and world cricket across three decades. He was feared by opposing teams, respected by his critics, admired by his colleagues and worshipped by his fans. This was a man who didn't know the meaning of the word defeat and through his personal effort inspired his teammates to success when defeat seemed a foregone conclusion. Ian Botham deserves his award and is recognised internationally as a true legend in his own sport. The legendary all-rounder played 102 Tests for England, amassed 383 Test Wickets and 5200 runs during his illustrious career. Ian was, without doubt, a controversial character who spoke his mind and followed up his words with actions that typified the bulldog spirit that made him who he was.

At the end of his sporting career, that same spirit drove "Beefy" to new challenges: walking the length and breadth of the country to raise millions of pounds for children suffering with leukaemia and leukaemia research. Botham is a winner and an inspiration in every sense of the word and thoroughly deserves his Lifetime Achievement award.

The main event of the evening was for the BBC Sports Personality of the Year. This award went to a woman who epitomizes how the power of desire can help you overcome all obstacles to achieve your dream.

On the night, Kelly Holmes revealed that she had only ever had two goals in her life. The first was to become a physical training instructor (PTI) in the British Army and the second was to become an Olympic champion. Kelly achieved the first of her goals many years before but at thirty-four, the odds of her achieving her Olympic dream seemed remote. The twelve-year-old Kelly showed great potential, but seven of her eleven years as a full-time athlete were beset with problems of illness and injury.

We don't see the heartache, the tears and the breaking down. We don't witness the frustrations and the mental and physical suffering that injury and illness causes. We had no idea of the sacrifices that Kelly had made over those eleven years in order to achieve her dream. Most of us would have caved in and conceded defeat a long time before the Athens Olympics arrived.

But Kelly is very different from the majority. Her ambition, focus and desire would never allow her to give up. I have followed Kelly's career for many years watching her progress then suffer setbacks on the verge of greatness. But what I saw in Athens during her heat of the 800 metres was a very different Kelly: her focus was startling. Standing on the starting line, she exhibited no emotion just sheer concentration and total focus on the job ahead. Kelly won the race easily but at the end there was no sharing of handshakes, no smiles, no interaction with her competitors. Kelly crossed the line still focused, very serious and left the track immediately. She behaved the same in every race and, as each stage of the 800 metres took place, people began to sense that they were in the presence of a champion.

The rest is history: Kelly out-sprinted Mozambique's Maria Mutola to win the Olympic final of the 800 metres. It was only on the line that Kelly could finally express the emotion of the occasion. It was clear to see the realisation that a lifetime of effort and dedication had finally been rewarded with the achievement of Kelly's second lifetime goal – the Olympic medal.

Kelly went on to run the 1500 metres and glided into the land of the legends by surpassing her own dreams and becoming a double Olympic champion.

Anything is possible if you want it bad enough – just ask Kelly.

Although not the main award of the evening, I've purposely kept it until last.

This award is called the Helen Rollason Award in memory of the BBC's sports presenter, Helen Rollason, and is given for showing courage in adversity.

This very special award pays tribute to very special people. The award in 2004 went to a young woman called Kirsty Howard. Kirsty at only nine years old was terminally ill. Kirsty couldn't walk without the aid of oxygen and spent most of her time in a wheelchair.

Her charity, Kirsty's Appeal, had already raised three million pounds for sick children.

Kirsty had an inoperable heart condition having been born with her heart back to front. Despite being given just six weeks to live in 1999, Kirsty battled on to touch the hearts of millions, including some of the world's most famous sports stars, such as David Beckham and Sir Alex Ferguson.

Despite her suffering, Kirsty has demonstrated tremendous courage and has spent most of her life to date raising money for other children. Her strength, despite her severe illness, has inspired millions. Kirsty attends major sporting events to publicise her work and raise the profile of her charity.

She famously stole the nation's heart two years ago when, clutching David Beckham's hand, she presented the baton to the Queen at the Commonwealth Games.

In 2004 when the young girl walked into the BBC studio aided by her nurse, wheeling her oxygen supply behind her, I don't think there was a dry eye in the place. Kirsty was not a sporting legend, but she received the only standing ovation of the evening. The sporting superstars were in awe of this very brave young girl who displayed enormous courage, an unbroken spirit and the same never give-up attitude that turns ordinary people into living legends.

Ian Botham, Gary Lineker, Jensen Button, Arsene Wenger, Sven Goram Eriksson, Boris Becker, Kelly Holmes, Matthew Pinsent, Maurice Greene, Amir Khan and the whole of the international audience stood together and paid tribute to a very special young woman.

What a fantastic evening. There were so many inspiring stories of human greatness concentrated into one gala event. The message from the occasion is very simple: every one of the people in that studio, including the courageous Kirsty, had dreams. They all had stories to tell regarding their own personal challenges but they never allowed setbacks of any nature prevent them from realising their ambitions and making their dreams come true.

Their desire remained strong, although tested to the limits, and the sacrifice was immense, but that's the price winners are prepared to pay in order to elevate themselves into real champions.

When we think about sporting superstars or courageous young girls like Kirsty McKenzie, take some inspiration and start to focus on your own goals:

⇨ Professional
⇨ Spiritual
⇨ Social
⇨ Family
⇨ Educational

Things to do:

⇨ Decide what it is important to you.

> Things that are vitally important are not always what you want but more about what you need. You may want to live in a mansion but realistically what you need in the first instance is to provide a safe home for your family. The mansion can come later once the basic provision and security has been put in place.

⇨ Read 'Human Motivations' by **Abraham Harold Maslow**. Maslow (April 1, 1908 – June 8, 1970) was an American psychologist who was best known for creating Maslow's hierarchy of needs, a theory of self-actualization.

The best way to explain this principle is to make reference to Abraham Maslow's work:

Maslow developed the theory of human motivation now known as Maslow's Hierarchy of Needs. A psychologist, Maslow noted that some human needs were more powerful than others. He divided those needs into five general categories, from most urgent to most advanced: physiological, safety, belonging/love, esteem, and self-actualisation. Maslow first published his theory in the 1940s, and it became a widely accepted notion in the fields of psychology and anthropology.

According to Maslow, there are general types of needs (physiological, safety, love, and esteem) that must be satisfied before a person can act unselfishly. He called these needs "deficiency needs." As long as we are motivated to satisfy these cravings, we are moving towards growth, toward self-actualisation. Satisfying needs is healthy; blocking gratification makes us sick or evil. In other words, we are all "needs junkies" with cravings that must be satisfied and should be satisfied.

Maslow's Hierarchy of Needs is illustrated as a triangle...

The model is triangular because as you move up the scale, fewer and fewer people manage to satisfy the higher level of needs.

We begin at the first / bottom level...

Physiological needs – Man needs food to eat, air to breathe, water to drink, and heat for warmth. These are the basic necessities of survival. These are Man's first and most important needs.

Physiological Needs

Physiological needs are the very basic needs such as air, water, food, sleep, sex, etc. When these are not satisfied we may feel sickness, irritation, pain, discomfort, etc. These feelings motivate us to alleviate them as soon as possible to establish homeostasis. Once they are alleviated, we may think about other things.

Second level...

Safety – Man needs a place to live that protects him from the elements and predators.

Safety Needs

Safety needs have to do with establishing stability and consistency in a chaotic world. These needs are mostly psychological in nature. We need the security of a home and family. Many in our society cry out for law and order because they do not feel safe enough to go for a walk in their community. In addition, safety needs sometimes motivate people to be religious. Religions comfort us with the promise of a safe secure place after we die and leave the insecurity of this world.

Third level...

We meet our social and belonging needs i.e. we find partners or join groups of friends, etc.

Love Needs

Love and belongingness is the next level. Humans have a desire to belong to groups: clubs, work groups, religious groups, family, gangs, etc. We need to feel loved (non-sexual) by others, to be accepted by others. Performers and entertainers appreciate applause. We as human beings need to be needed.

Fourth Level...

Esteem – you achieve something that provides recognition and personal satisfaction such as an academic achievement or award.

Esteem Needs

There are two types of esteem needs. First is self-esteem, which results from competence or mastery of a task. You feel good about yourself and what you have achieved. Then there's the attention and recognition that comes from others. This is similar to the belonging level, however, seeking admiration or approval from others, signifies the desire for authority and the need for power. People, who have all of their lower needs satisfied, often drive very expensive cars because doing so raises their level of esteem.

Fifth Level...

Self-actualisation – achieved by the few. Normally this is the first person to do something spectacular: Roger Bannister in 1954 was the first person to run a four minute mile. His time was 3.59.04. The following year fifty more people achieved this target but Bannister was the first. He self-actualised as the first person to run sub- four minutes.

Self-Actualisation

The need for self-actualisation is having a desire to become and achieve one or more of your dreams. People who have security of their basic needs can focus their energies on fulfilling their potential, the dream is achieved and self-actualisation takes place.

The Model...

It is a little simplistic but succeeds in introducing the concept of differing needs within human beings.

Maslow's study focuses on the needs of individuals and tells us clearly that if the need is strong enough people will do everything within their power to satisfy it. Once that need is satisfied you move on to the next level of needs. This process is the same as 'goal setting'. You have a dream, you focus on a strategy to achieve that dream and when successful, you move on to the next challenge.

Kelly Holmes achieved her dream to win Olympic gold by winning the 800 metres in Athens. Once this was achieved Kelly moved on to the next challenge and within days won her second Olympic gold in the 1500 metres.

⇨ Take a sheet of paper and write down all of those things that you currently "need".

⇨ Split your needs into categories for a proper work / life balance. It is no good focusing on achieving something professionally and then losing your family in the process because you simply didn't have time for them – remember the story of the "Mexican fisherman". Use the following categories for help:

> ⟩ Spiritual
> ⟩ Social
> ⟩ Family
> ⟩ Educational

⇨ Set timescales against each of the needs. These needs become your top priorities. If you don't achieve them within the timescale, don't worry, simply reschedule and adjust your focus and strategy.

⇨ Kelly Holmes didn't become Olympic champion until she was thirty-four. Despite setbacks Kelly did not give up – you must not contemplate giving up your dreams.

⇨ Tell someone about your plans. This puts gentle pressure on you to achieve what you've committed to.

⇨ Once you've set out a strategy for your needs, repeat the exercise for your wants. These are your dreams – dreams are goal-focused.

➩ Don't create too many goals. You need focus. Remember Kelly Holmes only had two goals outside her needs: PTI in the Army and Olympic champion. If you focus on a few goals, you're more likely to achieve them.

➩ Start to see problems that occur along your journey as challenges. This will help you fully appreciate the true value of achieving your goals.

➩ Have faith and believe in yourself. You are a special person. Anything is possible if you believe. Henry Ford once said, "If you believe you can you can and if you believe you can't you can't."

Setting yourself goals is taking yourself seriously – simply taking a real interest in you. Your life is important, so realise your full potential and make your dreams become reality. Stop thinking about what you might achieve and start to plan how you can make your desires come true. Believe you can. Never, ever give up, and never become distracted by other people's comments or opinions. Follow your heart and trust your instincts and the sheer power of your desires will lead you to your dreams.

17.

Exceed expectation levels

Exceed expectation levels

Learn to manage expectation levels. Start with your own. Why allow yourself to become disappointed with what life throws at you? This might seem to contradict the points made in the previous chapter, 'Set new challenges and goals' but you will see that this is not the case.

You continue to set goals, you still have dreams and the process for achievement stays the same, but you manage your expectations along the way. That way, when setbacks, disappointment and adversity strike, you are mentally prepared to deal with them and move on.

Kelly Holmes the British middle distance runner and double Olympic gold medallist at the Athens Olympics had set herself clear goals. One of those goals was to become the Olympic champion, but the fact that she became double Olympic champion by winning gold at the 800 and 1500 metre events, exceeded her own expectations.

The sooner we realise that there are no guarantees in life the more content we become. We must always strive to do our best, to achieve what we can, but this must be balanced with contentment and an appreciation of what you currently have.

For example the next time it rains, don't complain about it – go out and walk in it! Enjoy it for what it is. Rain doesn't hurt you, it makes you wet, but so what? Get wet and enjoy the experience of getting wet.

If you expect every day of your life to be filled with glorious sunshine then you will be sadly disappointed, so make the most of what you have. Enjoy the rain and you will be amazed with the experience and, when it does eventually stop raining and the sun comes out, you will feel so much better because your expectation levels of happiness have been exceeded.

With the right attitude to the things in life that you have no control over, you will feel more relaxed and better mentally equipped to deal with the challenges.

It's the same with your family, friends and in business – your customers. You must learn to manage their expectation levels or risk the possibility of them becoming disappointed in you.

It's always very wise to be honest with people and under-promise so that you can over-deliver. Here are some examples:

Your wife asks you to be home by seven pm to look after the kids, so she can visit a friend. You agree but turn up at six. She'll be very impressed with how you listened, took her seriously and cared enough to exceed her expectations.

A customer orders an item from your business and asks when it will be delivered. You say that the normal delivery is up to seven working days. The customer accepts and you actually deliver within three.

The customer is delighted. You have exceeded his expectation level and he tells the world what a wonderful company you are and what a great service you provide.

Your son asks you to take him to a local football match. You agree but you also know he is a keen Manchester United supporter. You take him to the local football match and while you are there, surprise him with tickets to watch his favourite team play Chelsea in a few week's time.

He is ecstatic at the thought of visiting one of the best football stadiums in the world and watching his heroes play live. You have exceeded his expectation level and he thinks you're the best dad in the world.

Things to do:

➩ Manage your own expectation levels.

➩ Walk in the rain and splash in a puddle – get wet!

➩ Accept that life offers no guarantees and you'll find it easier to deal with life's challenges.

➩ Learn to manage the expectation levels of others by carefully listening to their needs.

➩ Always under-promise then over-deliver.

⇨ If you over-promise and under-deliver, then re-build your credibility. Start by apologising profusely.

⇨ Enjoy the moment when your expectations are exceeded – such moments are rare.

⇨ Enjoy the happy and fulfilled reaction of others when you have exceeded their expectations.

⇨ Accept appreciation and gratitude graciously.

⇨ Use empathy to understand what it is you need to do in order to exceed people's expectations.

Human beings are very intelligent but more importantly extremely emotional. Expectation is an emotion. If you mismanage it you will draw a negative reaction. However, if you manage it well, you will create joy and happiness within yourself and a highly rewarding positive response from the person whose expectation levels have been exceeded.

People do business with people they like and trust and this becomes most effective when expectation levels are exceeded.

18.

Become a great networker

Become a great networker

What is networking? In its simplest form it can be regarded as socialising, people circulating and communicating with others. No matter how good you are at what you do, when you're not visible you're easily forgotten. Life goes on with or without you, so while you're here circulate and make the most of the opportunities that exist.

Let's remind ourselves again of Maslow's 'Hierarchy of Needs' and in particular the Third level:

Love Needs

Love and belongingness is the next level. Humans have a desire to belong to groups: clubs, work groups, religious groups, family, gangs, etc. We need to feel loved (non-sexual) by others, to be accepted by others. Performers and entertainers appreciate applause. We as human beings need to be needed.

So assuming Maslow is right, the benefits of networking are pretty obvious. As human beings we need to be a part of something and networking certainly helps us in that regard.

As I've mentioned before, people form relationships and friendships, and do business with people they like and trust. From a very young age we are networking at school, forming relationships with circles of friends and, as we grow older, that same process repeats itself in college, university and workplaces as well as social, religious, political and business clubs that we subscribe to.

Networking promotes you as a brand to all those who might be interested in you, while at the same time giving you the opportunity to seek out those people you want to be associated with.

Make the most of you and your life and seek the opportunities that exist by committing yourself to becoming a world-class networker.

Things to do:

⇨ Sharpen up your communication skills, practise listening and questioning techniques.

⇨ Remember to consistently wear your smile – sincerely. People like to be associated with happy people.

⇨ Decide which groups – professional and social – you want to be involved with. Make contact and ask how you get involved.

⇨ Prepare a great introduction or 'elevator speech' so that when people ask who you are and what you do, you're fully prepared with a direct and interesting answer. You only have one opportunity to make a great first impression.

⇨ Empathy is always a great quality to have in networking situations. Put yourself in the shoes of those you are attempting to make contact with and ask yourself the question: "What would I be thinking if I were them?" If you get this right you'll make a connection.

⇨ If in business always carry plenty of business cards.

⇨ Always network with successful people. Why? You can learn and develop by listening to people who have been there, done it and have the results to prove it.

⇨ Circulate. When you enter a room where there are a lot of people, spend your time circulating from person to person. Listen and promote you, as a brand, at every opportunity. A word of warning – do not become overpowering.

⇨ When circulating within large groups, three or four minutes is a good time to be in conversation with someone before moving on. Always be courteous, introduce others to the group you're in, and always ask politely if it's OK for you to join a new group before introducing yourself, and then tune in to the conversation.

⇨ Subscribe to on-line newsletters relevant to your interests.

⇨ Start to build your own database and think about creating a newsletter for your peer group.

⇨ Don't stand on the sidelines in public, observe the actions of those in the room. Find a person who is on their own or a group of three or more. Avoid interrupting two people talking unless invited or you know them well – they could be in the middle of a very important conversation.

⇨ Seek out and approach people you want to speak with. If they're in a group, hover until the moment is right, and then begin the conversation by asking, "May I join you?" Don't forget they are also networking so it's unlikely they will say no. If they do, they might not be people you want to associate with anyway so simply move on.

⇨ Keep smiling and always make sure your body language and eye contact is positive.

⇨ When you engage in conversation, remember to ask open-ended questions to find out as much as you can about the person you are speaking to – this will demonstrate your interest in them. Believe it or not, this is the art of a great conversationalist.

Like anything in life, networking gets better with practice. The more you do, the more confident and successful you become as a networker. The most successful social and business relationships are usually formed through networking and you will often find that successful people are great networkers renowned for their social skills and their ability to interact with others.

The good news is that if you're not already an accomplished networker, there is no reason at all why you can't become one very quickly. Take on board the action points listed above and start networking today. Pick up the phone, send an email or subscribe to a club, association or professional body that you are interested in. Don't think about it – just do it. You'll be pleasantly surprised at the progress you make.

19.

Become a great conversationalist

Become a great conversationalist

What makes a great conversationalist? It's a myth that it's a person who always has something to say. Like everyone, I enjoy listening to interesting people who have great stories and experiences to share, but I also become very frustrated with people who talk incessantly about themselves without any regard for the other person.

The art of great conversation is to encourage two-way communication and the only way to do this is to ask the right kind of interesting questions. To give you an idea of what I mean, tune into the Oprah Winfrey Show or watch the Parkinson Show.

Michael Parkinson is a great conversationalist regarded by many as the best in his field because he gets his guests to open up and talk about themselves. His skill is in probing their responses to his questions, which means he steers and remains in total control of the conversation.

It's not only the verbal communication which is important, it's the sincerity in your voice. People know when you're listening and when you're not. Your body language is essential. You can display the fact that you're interested and listening by smiling, maintaining eye contact and making gestures such as nodding your head in acknowledgement. It's no good pretending to be interested, you have to physically show it in order to become a great conversationalist.

Leaning in towards people as you ask questions, rather than standing rigidly with crossed arms, demonstrates openness and encourages people to communicate with you in a friendly way.

The real skill of all good conversationalists is to listen carefully to the beginning, middle and end of the other person's sentences. Take in every point, clarify where necessary and then probe for more information. When all the information you require is clear, respond with clarity and friendliness, varying the pitch and tone in your voice to put key points across in an emphatic and interesting way.

Use the power of silence to create impact. Speed up the conversation to energise and create excitement, then slow it down again to check that people haven't misunderstood what you're saying.

Things to do:

⇨ Listen to great conversationalists in action. Watch Oprah, Jeremy Paxman or Michael Parkinson and study their techniques.

⇨ Teach yourself to become a great listener. Pay attention to the entire conversation including the beginning and the end – very often the most important part.

⇨ Always listen out for people's names, remember them – and address them by their names. You will be amazed at the reaction you get. Ask open-ended questions to encourage conversation. Begin each question using one of the ever dependable and useful '5 W's and an H':

> Who…
> What…
> Where…
> Why…
> When…
> How…

⇨ Once you've asked open-ended questions, listen to the response and then probe the answers.

⇨ Build rapport. Smile, use eye contact and be friendly.

⇨ Be empathetic. Put yourself in the shoes of the other person and make a connection.

⇨ Be passionate about you and your subject.

⇨ Listen and speak with enthusiasm.

⇨ Avoid sarcasm and cynicism. Be seen as a positive person.

⇨ Be you. Be sincere.

Conversation is an art. People who practise the art of conversation have a genuine interest in other people. This sets them apart from those whose self-involved conversation might reflect a shallow personality and insecurity.

Great conversationalists are different; they genuinely care about others and that sincerity comes across in their body language and the tone of voice. Be interesting, listen, probe and respond with passion, to become a master of the art of conversation.

20.

Have a great introduction

Have a great introduction

You meet someone socially for the very first time and they ask you what you do. You're at a formal event and you are introduced to lots of different people (a networking opportunity) who ask you what you do. You finally get the opportunity to speak to the person you've been admiring for some time and, as the conversation develops, they ask, "What do you do?" You're at a dinner party and people ask you what you do. You're in a lift (elevator) and the key decision maker who you've been targeting as a potential business opportunity steps inside. You begin a conversation and they ask, "What is it that you do?"

So what is it that you do? The challenge is for you to tell the questioner exactly that, and, more importantly, how it may benefit them. In addition, you need to you express yourself with clarity, energy and in a way that conveys a positive message to the listener within a very short space of time.

Every day brings new opportunities socially and professionally, but those opportunities are easily lost if you fail to make the right impression on the very people providing those opportunities. I make no apology for repeating the statement: *"People build relationships or do business with people who they like and trust"*. The first part of that process is the initial impression you make when you come into contact with new people.

Although people will tune in to what you have to say, they might tune out just as quickly if they are not inspired or find you uninteresting. So your challenge in the communication process is on three fronts:

1. Look good. Be confident. Be attractive to other people.
2. Think carefully about what you intend to say. Be prepared.
3. Say it with purpose, conviction and passion.

The first challenge is to be confident in your appearance. In previous chapters we mentioned the need to love yourself and to be at ease with who you are and what you do. If you're at ease with yourself, your confidence will grow. Confident people carry presence and that is expressed through their body language, essential in the communication process and effective before you've spoken a single word.

The next stage is what you say. First rule: be sure about what you want to say, be precise and to the point. Make sure the point creates sufficient impact to make people interested enough to keep listening. Avoid waffle, stuttering or rambling as this switches off the listener within seconds.

Here's an example:

Your business is selling medical supplies. You're at a business event and are introduced to a potential new customer, a buyer working in primary care in the UK medical industry. The buyer, someone you have been planning to speak with for some time, asks you what you do. You need to tell them precisely and with clarity within twenty seconds – after that your impact is beginning to wane. You could use an introduction that goes like this:

"My name is Michael and I'm in medical supplies which help general practitioners provide the very best medical services for their patients. Would you like me to explain how I can help you do the same for your patients?"

Your explanation is concise and to the point and consists of no more than two sentences, and you can communicate this message in under ten seconds. What you're doing is buying time and creating a hook so that the listener gets a taste and will, hopefully, give you the go-ahead to expand on what you do and how your services can be of benefit to them.

In the 21st century everything happens at great speed and especially in business, time is precious. If you can communicate what you do with impact in a very short space of time, then you'll be different from the majority and you'll be successful in business.

Things to do:

➪ Start to believe in you, respect who you are and what you stand for.

➪ Practise your body language. Walk upright with shoulders back. Be aware of your eye contact and keep smiling.

➪ Write down a series of short introductions about you and what you do.

➪ Keep the introductions short and to the point.

⇨ Make sure the introductions say:

> ❭ Who you are, your name and company name if necessary.

> ❭ What you do and what business you are in.

> ❭ What's in it for the customer? How you can help them.

⇨ Select an introduction that you're most comfortable with and then practise repeating it until it becomes an automatic response.

⇨ When people ask you what you do, tell them with energy and passion.

⇨ Make them want to do business or be acquainted with you because of your conviction and passion.

⇨ Remember the rules of conversation. Get them talking as soon as you can by asking open-ended questions.

⇨ Remember the line: "First Impression – Great Impression – Every Time".

Finally, the key is to remember that your introduction is designed to create a great impression and buy you more time in the conversation. However, the ultimate success will depend on what questions you ask because you need to get the listener talking about themselves rather than listening to you. Remember the points raised in the previous chapter on great conversationalists and the need to establish two-way communication. These are essential if you are to continue beyond the initial introduction and develop your conversation towards a meaningful conclusion.

21.

Develop a great attitude

Focus on being the best at what you do

Develop a great attitude

Focus on being the best at whatever you do

Anyone involved in selling will tell you that a key characteristic associated with successful salespeople is a PMA, better known as a "Positive Mental Attitude".

But this isn't unique to sales or business, it applies to everyone and dictates how well we perform in most aspects of our daily lives.

Some people will feel uncomfortable at the very mention of this term, others claim to adopt a positive mental attitude at key moments, while a small percentage don't need to claim anything, they simply know no different: they perform to the highest possible standards every minute of every day, as born winners do.

For those who are feeling sceptical, I hope you'll read on because the truth is nobody is born into this world programmed to be a loser, circumstances of life tend to determine outcomes for the majority of people.

In many cases painful experiences affect people's confidence and self-belief so they start to believe that, given the choice between something positive or negative happening to them, the latter is most likely to occur.

But it genuinely doesn't have to be this way. As most successful people will tell you, they too have experienced such negative challenges at some stage in their lives and, during adversity, have managed to draw upon an inner strength to guide them above and beyond the 'pain barrier'.

History is littered with such examples:

Nelson Mandela spent most of his life in a South African prison but not even total isolation could break his spirit or alter his desire to achieve freedom and equality for all South Africans.

Martin Luther King inspired millions with his, "I have a dream…" vision, while Muhammad Ali began telling people he was "the greatest…" long before he was anywhere near greatness. Despite suffering with Parkinson's disease for the last twenty-five years, Ali continues to tell people he's the greatest and to dare anyone to challenge his claim!

In modern day sport, attitude is apparent among the top personalities. Tiger Woods, David Beckham, Michael Schumacher, Alex Ferguson Bradley Wiggins and Serena Williams are all typical examples of winners with a massive desire for unlimited success.

The simple fact is that we all have attitude and there is little difference in attitudes from person to person. The deciding factor is whether or not the attitude within is negative or positive.

People like to be associated with success stories whether in sport, history or modern day business, and success stories originate from successful people. Such people adopt the "Can do", "Will Try" approaches rather than the "Can't do", "Won't try". There is an old saying which I've heard on many occasions and which really illustrates this point:

"Give me a person with an average ability but with an enormous desire to succeed and I will make him a winner every time".
This is so true in every walk of life and separates the winners from the losers.

In reality we are what we are; very few of us are born into success. Success is what we make it and how we measure it depends on our performance against the goals we set ourselves in everyday life. However, the journey is very often determined by our attitude and how we deal with the challenges that come our way – whether we interpret them as obstacles or as another opportunity waiting to happen.

So there you have it – attitude. A little word that can make a big difference! The choice is yours and the odds are well in your favour. With a "fifty-fifty" chance, all you have to do is choose the positive option and enjoy the impact it will make to your life.

Good luck along your journey and remember it is you who can make the difference, so go and make it happen today!

Complete the Attitude Test.

There is very little difference between individuals. The little difference is attitude, the big impact comes from it being negative or positive. What is yours?

In any performance environment there are periods when nothing ever seems to go your way:

⇨ You might be in sales and you miss your target, or a major account cancels unexpectedly.

⇨ A customer you've known for some time calls to complain about poor service and delivery at the point when you thought your procedures and logistics were finely tuned.

⇨ A key person hands in their notice when you thought you had finished piecing together a well-balanced team.

Unexpected adversity and challenges have a habit of appearing just when you think everything is going swimmingly. Suddenly a thunderbolt hits, or, as a colleague of mine used to say in a busy advertising sales department, "And the hits keep coming!"

So how do you deal with it? Do you give up and walk away? Do you allow your emotions to drive negative behaviour? Or do you take on board the challenge, accept the responsibility and face up to the prospect of turning adversity into opportunity?

The following self-analysis test will give you ideas for coping in certain situations. It will tell you something about your state of mind and let you be the judge over whether your attitude is positive or negative.

1. You have just made a poor sales presentation to a potential customer. You know it was poor as you were in his company for only five minutes. He said very little, you talked a lot. He looked completely disinterested with what you had to say. What would you do?

   a. Accept it, move on and hope that, by luck rather than judgement, your next appointment will be better.

   b. Try and prepare more carefully next time around.

   c. Speak about the call with your sales manager and seek advice about how you can perfect your questioning skills to improve interaction with the customer.

2. A colleague at work criticises you openly during a team meeting. The subject of conversation is work-related but it is also feels personal to the point that you feel hurt and slightly betrayed. How will you react?

   a. You control your emotions and reply logically, explaining your actions in relation to the work-related subject.

   b. You struggle to disguise your fury and react aggressively.

   c. You bury your head in the sand and hope that other members of the team will spring to your defence.

3. You've just been called into a meeting with your manager to discuss your performance. This is the second month in succession that you've missed the target. There are reasons (there always are) for the shortfall, but your manager is not interested and demands a better performance during the month ahead. What is your response likely to be?

   a. You spend the next 20 minutes discussing the shortfall, debating the reasons and discussing possible solutions with your manager.

   b. You openly demonstrate your resentment of the criticism.

   c. You say nothing in response but complain bitterly to your colleagues about your manager outside the meeting.

4. A customer has written a letter of complaint. The content criticises service levels including the time taken to deal with their initial phone call, the attitude of the member of staff they were dealing with and the time taken to deliver the product, which when it did arrive was the incorrect item! You are the person who took the enquiry and processed the order. What would you do?

   a. Telephone or write to the customer defending your actions and challenging the allegations made against you.

   b. Replace the incorrect items immediately and make an appointment with the customer to discuss the matter in detail.

   c. Correct the order and contact the customer to inform them of your actions.

5. A colleague in another department, but in the same building as yourself sends you an email criticising the way you carried out a certain procedure and demands that you don't repeat the same again. You are convinced that their demands are both wrong and unreasonable. In fact you are convinced that it is they, rather than you, who have abused the procedure. How do you react?

   a. You send an email back explaining your own actions, suggesting that your colleague needs to re-look at the procedure.

   b. You complain to your manager.

   c. You take time out to understand the issue, making a point of visiting your colleague to discuss what might have gone wrong and how it can best be resolved.

6. Things are not quite right at home. You are under immense pressure and right now the last place you need to be is at work. Do you?

   a. Try to keep your emotions to yourself and get on with work as though there was nothing wrong.

   b. Take out your frustrations on your colleagues, making life unbearable for all those around you.

   c. Say nothing, but your manner and appearance reveals to others that something isn't right.

7. Your boss has asked you to complete a report on your sector of the business. The report is for the next strategy meeting which takes place in two days' time. This is very short notice and you will have to work extremely hard over long hours to complete it in time. You produce the report and you know it is of a high standard. Your boss accepts it without a thank you or even a gesture of appreciation for your efforts. What is your reaction?

   a. You say nothing but tell your colleagues about your boss's behaviour.

   b. You sulk and allow it to affect your attitude towards your boss over the days and weeks ahead.

   c. You simply move on, knowing full well you did a great a job within a deadline.

8. You upset a colleague by accusing them of failing to complete a task which they had previously agreed to do. You are furious because it reflects badly on you. Your colleague is upset because they feel they've done everything that was asked of them. Later you realise that you mistakenly delegated to your colleague only half of the original task. What do you do?

   a. Pretend it didn't happen but make an effort in the future to be much more polite to your colleague.

   b. Pull them to one side and apologise profusely.

   c. Discuss the incident with others before taking a course of action.

9. You are regarded as one of the best performers in the team. This reputation has been earned through consistent results over the last two years. Suddenly your performance falls below the usual standard, your confidence is affected and for the first time others can identify that you're feeling the pressure. What is your reaction?

   a. You battle on hoping that matters will resolve themselves.

   b. You start looking for another job.

   c. You stand back, take stock, seek advice and put in place a plan to get you back on track.

10. Your company offers you an opportunity to visit their sister operation in Australia to help on a project for a month. This is a great opportunity to show your intentions within the organisation and a potential springboard for future promotion. What will you do?

    a. Thank them for the opportunity but decline on the basis of domestic commitments.

    b. Accept the invitation and focus your energy on making it a success.

    c. Request a further meeting to discuss the idea in more detail and then seek a period of time to consider your decision.

How to score your answers:

Where you have selected the following answers award yourself 10 points:

1. "C"	2. "A"
3. "A"	4. "B"
5. "C"	6. "A"
7. "C"	8. "B"
9. "C"	10. "B"

Score 80 to 100

You are an asset to your organisation. You are self-confident, disciplined and you have a real empathy with managers, peers and customers. You are committed to business goals and delivering service. You see adversity as a challenge and you have tremendous belief in your ability to deliver top quality performance on a consistent basis.

Score 50 to 70

You are a steady performer within the organisation. Your attitude overall is pretty good and you like to do the right thing. Sometimes when things aren't going your way you can be distracted by other people and unexpected situations which causes you to lose sight of the end goal. You need to be more confident in your own ability to deliver a better performance. Improved results will eventually lead to new confidence and a real belief in your own value to the organisation.

Score 10 to 40

You have difficulty remaining positive. You have a tendency to be cynical about situations that other people would view in a good way and you tend to look for hidden agendas that might not exist. It would appear you don't particularly like your job and you need to uncover what is causing the dissatisfaction with your current role. Unless you conquer your negative feelings your behaviour will undermine the potential good you have to offer.

Score less than 10

You need to take a long, hard look at what is behind your current inability to see beyond the negative. Don't despair, there are plenty of ways you can help yourself gain a more positive attitude. I hope that this book and other sources listed in the bibliography at the end, will provide you with ideas and ways to make those changes.

22.

Contribute to
your community

Contribute to your community

We all enjoy receiving gifts, compliments, good service and appreciation in whatever form it is given, but people often gain more satisfaction from giving than receiving. There is nothing more rewarding than seeing the reaction on someone's face when you've given them something special – you've shown you care.

Without beating the religion drum in any way, it's worth mentioning that some of the readings in The Bible have great meaning and if practised in everyday life help us to be more understanding of one another and more supportive of 'community' in a local and global sense. I suppose what I'm trying to say relates back to those famous biblical words, "Love thy neighbour".

I grew up in a working class mining community in the south Wales valleys. At its peak there were three operational coal mines in our village. Despite the poor working conditions and a typical working class wage in return, the overall community spirit was immense.

People very rarely left the village; everything they needed was there including work, church, chapel, the local Co-operative store which supplied everything you could possibly dream of, together with local butchers, hardware stores, Italian cafés, pubs, working men's clubs and institutes, betting offices (turf accountants) barber shops, grocers, bakers and local farmers who supplied everything from dairy products, to vegetables, to the meat on the table.

Very few families had cars, primarily because they couldn't afford them but also because they were unnecessary as people very rarely left their community. People worked hard seven days a week and the small amount of free time was spent with family and friends in the local community.

The streets were safe: children played outside without fear from early in the morning until the evening and held total respect for the community and its way of life. If we stepped out of line we were quickly reprimanded by a parent, relative or whichever adult was there to witness our misbehaviour. If that didn't work the local bobby (policeman) gave us a good talking-to. There was no need for any further action after that.

The coal mines were the hub of the community. They created the shared wealth which allowed people to stay local and earn enough money to support their family needs. Values were high and, in a Christian community, church and chapel were an integral part of life: on a Sunday they were packed to the rafters with men, women and children paying their respects in accordance with the Christian faith.

Our house, although very basic, (no central heating, no refrigeration and a black and white TV) was a mid-terrace, three-up, two-down property and was always full of people. Grandparents, uncles, aunts, cousins and friends were in and out all day and every day as was typical of every other house in this close-knit community. The kettle was constantly on and the storytelling was fantastic! In the 21st century, I should remind you, that this is what is referred to as the dying art of conversation!

If someone fell ill the whole village knew about it and there was a stream of visitors offering sympathy and support in a time of need. If there was any trouble, the reaction was the same and if someone died, the whole village attended the funeral, paying their respects to the passing of one of their own.

When I write about this now it all sounds a little unreal and more like an imaginative dream. But it wasn't a dream.

Many would refer to these times as, "The Good Old Days" but let's not get carried away: these times were tough and I wouldn't want my reminiscences to discourage progress. I am simply describing those qualities that can make communities great. The experience was real and it was an example of 'community' working at its best with people who had very little material wealth giving something more valuable than money: their time.

It was an era when people found time for one another, when people supported their community and took pride in the basic human values. It is no coincidence that a large number of these people had experienced great suffering and loss in their lives. This was less than twenty years after the end of the Second World War and the rebuilding of the free world and an appreciation of freedom, was still fresh in people's minds.

I can talk freely about this subject because this was my personal experience of community life, but there are thousands of similar examples from across the world. Although time has moved on and lifestyles have changed, it is fundamentally important as a society to find time for others and the community. If we don't, we face a world in the future diminished by the loss of community values and the best of the human spirit.

It is something I strongly believe in and which I try to practise in my own life. I have a young family and I make sure that I get involved in school and community activities. My son is a Catholic and although I am not, I still make the effort to go with him to church because we are a Christian family and Christian values form the basis of our belief.

In addition, twice a week, I give up my time to coach a junior rugby team. It is rewarding and humbling to see young kids doing great things on the rugby field. They are proud of their achievements and in turn they make their parents proud of them. We have great fun as a team and we celebrate together at the end of each game. The community spirit certainly lives on in my part of the world – but, like life, you get out of it only what you are prepared to put in.

Things to do:

⇨ Re-evaluate your work-life balance. Decide what is important to you.

⇨ What are your values? What do you stand for? Practise your values in public so that people start to see the real you.

⇨ Take an interest in community affairs. Read your local newspaper and stay tuned to what's happening around you.

⇨ Acknowledge your neighbours. Smile at them, greet them by name every time you see them and make an effort to have a conversation.

⇨ Show real interest in your family, friends and neighbours. Ask questions about them and make time to listen to what they have to say.

⇨ Give up your time for free to support or organise community events, for example:

> Fundraise for local charities, local schools or hospitals.

> Organise a Community Fete for all the family.

⇨ If you are religious, attend and support your local church, mosque, synagogue or place of worship.

⇨ Join a local club and if you have children lend a hand with their activities:

> Help coach the kids at the local football or rugby club.

> Accompany the kids on Scout trips.

> Help organise events for the Brownies.

> Get involved in the local drama groups. If you're unable to act, help with the props, costumes, etc.

> Join community art groups – and have some fun!

⇨ Take an interest in local politics. Vote and have a say about your community. Better still why not stand for election as a community representative?

⇨ Get involved with local schools. Children are our future – pass on to them your words of wisdom – we all have something of value to offer.

Community or no community? We all have an opportunity to make a contribution. If we decide to isolate ourselves in our ivory towers then we have no right to complain about what goes on outside it. So take action and help make the difference by getting involved and making a contribution. In return, I can assure you from my personal experience, you will feel enormous satisfaction.

23.

Create a set
of values that
reflect you

Create a set of values that reflect you

What are values? We've spent a lot of time talking about the community in the previous chapter and I made a number of references to my own upbringing and the values that were passed onto me through my childhood by the people I respected and loved.

Values, put simply, represent who you are, what you are about and what you stand for. Knowing them is important but practising them is essential if you want to live the life you truly believe in.

A value could be described as a principle, quality or standard considered worthwhile. If you apply this to the things that you believe in, this will be apparent in everything that you do.

There are hundreds of individuals who have used values as the building blocks of their empires. There are bad examples and there are good ones. I choose to make reference only to the good ones, such as Mother Theresa who had no material wealth but dedicated her whole life to giving love to others – probably the most precious gift of all.

Then there's Nelson Mandela, whose beliefs and values, despite being locked away for twenty-five years of his life, inspired the South African people to force his release and replace apartheid with a democratic and free South Africa.

Closer to home, there was the great, British wartime leader, Winston Churchill, who inspired a nation to repel and, with the support of the Allies, defeat the Nazis to liberate the free world during the Second World War.

All three are legends in their own right who shared strong beliefs and values. As they went about their daily work, they sent clear messages to the people they pledged to serve and inspired positive change and hope in the process.

Back in the business world, I spoke once at a conference in London for a company called Armstrong World Wide Industries. Besides the more glamorous names such as Henry Ford and Walt Disney, I was personally inspired by the passion and beliefs of Armstrong's founder, Mr Thomas Morton Armstrong, who established the business in 1860.

I found reading the history of the business both inspiring and refreshing and it's a great example of how an individual's core values can shape the future of a business beyond their own lifetime.

Various changes and developments have taken place within Armstrong World Wide Industries since its formation as a company, which now spans three centuries. However, the company's leadership has adhered to Thomas Armstrong's central belief that his company's greatest asset is the people associated with the business -- its employees, customers and neighbours.

The following is an extract taken from Armstrong's corporate history. It is an extremely strong example of the importance of values:

Armstrong's founder, Thomas Morton Armstrong, turned the old business maxim Caveat emptor – "Let the buyer beware" – on its head and replaced it with five simple words, "Let The Buyer Have Faith".

Down through the years, the company has continued to prove itself worthy of that customer faith – through the respect shown to individuals in all its dealings; through the high moral and ethical standards consistently maintained; and in the integrity, reliability and forthrightness reflected in all its relationships.

When it all began in a tiny two-man cork-cutting shop in 1860 in Pittsburgh, our national frontier barely reached beyond the western mountain ranges. Thomas Armstrong's first deliveries of hand-carved corks were by wheelbarrow.

In the company's early days, Thomas Armstrong, the son of ordinary Scotch-Irish immigrants from Londonderry, steered his struggling company through the Civil War, financial panics, disastrous factory fires and a cutthroat marketplace.

He succeeded because he relied upon a family credo of hard work and faith. He attracted and held dedicated employees who shared the same values. He took pride in the production and sale of quality products that bore his family name. And he was determined that his company always act with fairness and in the "balanced best interests (of) customers, stockholders, employees, suppliers, community neighbours, government and the general public."

Down through the years, the company has continued to prove itself worthy of that customer faith – through the respect shown to individuals in all its dealings; through the high moral and ethical standards consistently maintained; and in the integrity, reliability and forthrightness reflected in all its relationships.

Today, five generations later, Armstrong is a worldwide family of 18,000 employees who manufacture and market a vast portfolio of branded products and services worldwide. Armstrong products include commercial and residential floor coverings and acoustical ceilings and grid systems and wood cabinets.

Key dates In Armstrong's Corporate History

1860: Opening of a small cork-cutting shop by Thomas Morton Armstrong in Pittsburgh, Pennsylvania.

1890: Armstrong is the largest cork company worldwide.

1900: Expansion to linoleum, ceiling board, vinyl floors, furniture, ceramic tiles...

1952: Opening of the Research and Development Centre in Lancaster.

1966: Opening of the first manufacturing unit in Europe (United Kingdom).

1996: Opening of the first manufacturing unit in Asia

1998: Acquisition of Triangle Pacific and DLW

2000: With the acquisition of Gema, a leading metal ceiling manufacturer in Europe, Armstrong offers custom solutions in metal

Today Armstrong is a worldwide family of 18,000 employees who manufacture and market hundreds of products.

The story of Armstrong confirms that solid values never date, they stand the test of time, outliving individuals and steering businesses in the right direction. Values cope with change and uncertainty, wars and depression, technology and changing markets. Values are the building blocks of society and business alike and will always succeed as long as they are believed and practised by the people they represent.

Things to do:

⇨ Decide who you are, what you believe in, what you want to do in life, and what you stand for.

⇨ Apply the above in business and in your private life.

⇨ When you have answered the above questions, write down your answers.

⇨ Learn your values so that you know them from the inside out.

⇨ More importantly practise being who you say you are and what you represent.

⇨ Encourage those around you to do the same.

⇨ Do business with people who share your values.

⇨ Encourage your staff to understand and practise your values. Although Walt Disney and Thomas Morton Armstrong are deceased their dreams live on through their people practising their values.

⇨ Understand integrity and service. Deliver what you say and serve all.

⇨ Don't rush into deciding your values. They are the building blocks of your future, so be sure that they are right for you.

24.

Embrace technology and change

Embrace technology and change

Don't resist it – embrace it! Change is constant, so go with it, have a positive attitude towards it; enjoy and take satisfaction from the learning experience that goes hand in hand with change.

The reason why people can find change so difficult is because it forces them to act and think outside their comfort zone. The tragedy is that change will happen with or without your buy-in, and unfortunately it's those people who attempt to resist it that so often become casualties.

In life we experience change from the moment we begin to develop in our mother's womb. Our minds and bodies develop and continue to change and adapt throughout our lifetime.

One could argue that this is where the change process terminates, but others believe that spiritually, the process continues beyond the grave.

Whatever your thoughts and beliefs, our time on this planet is spent dealing with the change and intense pace that life presents us with. This is why it seems so illogical to make yourself miserable at home or at work by resisting the development and change process as it unfolds before you.

This doesn't mean to say that you have to accept every new proposal, process or debate that comes your way. But it does mean that you should listen, keep an open mind and ask yourself what the potential benefits are that this change might bring.

In the business world, companies fold because they fall behind developments and new ways of doing things:

Competitors launching new products, or new processes allowing cheaper production might drive those companies which fail to respond to lose their customers and markets, resulting in eventual closure.

Cheap labour costs and huge technological developments in the Far East have forced Western businesses to reinvent themselves in order to compete. No longer is business restricted to local or national markets, indeed new technology has turned the 21st century into a global economy where the pace of change has moved into a new sphere. Those who fail to keep pace risk the danger of falling so far behind that they simply cease to become attractive or competitive to the customers they depend on.

At a time when this rate of change is so intense, values and morals become even more important. As human beings we have a moral obligation to consider and help those less fortunate than ourselves, irrespective of race, culture or creed. The rich Western countries of the world have a moral obligation to use their wealth to assist and help those developing countries educate, train and invest in their people, so that the gap between the rich and the poor recedes rather increases.

The 2004 tsunami in South East Asia was a terrible reminder of how frail the human race is when Mother Nature unleashes her frightening power.

In the space of seven days the death toll grew from a few thousand local people to a global catastrophe where over a hundred and fifty thousand people lost their lives. The scale of destruction that decimated areas of land in Indonesia, Sri Lanka, India, Africa, Thailand and hundreds of islands in the Indian Ocean was unimaginable before newsreels began to transmit the real horror in the final days of the year.

As horrific and tragic as the whole event was, it is heartening and encouraging to see the speed and willingness of the world to come together to help one another. Chinese, Americans, Europeans, Arabs, Africans, Japanese, Australians, Black, White, Yellow, Christian, Moslem, Buddhist and Jews all worked together with one heart to help those affected by the horror and tragedy in the aftermath of the tsunami.

In a bizarre twist, adversity on this occasion forced governments and nations to change the way they view our world and the people who live on this wonderful planet. It is amazing the progress that is made when politics are put to one side and man decides to work as one to benefit all. Technology, manpower and resources are brought together to provide vital support for those in need.

Let us hope that we learn from such catastrophic events and that we can use the same technology, resources and will to work together to overcome our cultural and political differences, and build a better and safer world for our children.

Things to do:

⇨ Be positive about change. Look for the potential good brought by change rather than the bad.

⇨ Change is constant but remember, you always have a choice. Sticking to your core values will help you make the right decisions in your personal and professional life.

⇨ Re-evaluate your values. Believe in your values and practise what you preach.

⇨ Sign up to a lifetime of learning as set out in the first four chapters. This will develop you as a person and show you the positive potential benefits associated with change and development.

⇨ Always consider the impact of any change you impose on others. Be empathetic to their situation and be fair.

⇨ Be honest with all those people affected by change which you instigate.

⇨ Embrace technology. There are real benefits including enhanced communication, understanding our planet and its natural resources, and medical breakthroughs that can save the lives of millions.

⇨ Respect change. You will not always agree with certain changes, but understand the positives as well as the negatives and show respect.

⇨ Do not allow change to disrupt the balance in your life. Before you sign up to anything, make sure that your work-life balance stays intact.

⇨ Use your new-found skills and experience gained from changes in your life to help others less fortunate or less experienced, have the opportunity to achieve the same.

⇨ As the world changes always try to give more than you take.

Use the above action points to become a pioneer for positive change. Inspire others to see the opportunities that exist and encourage those around you to realize their desires and achieve their goals. Be seen as a wise and visionary person, optimistic about the future while not losing sight of traditional values that demonstrate your respect for all of those around you.

25.

Find yourself a coach or mentor

Find yourself a coach or mentor

No matter how good you are you can always get better. Repeated practice will certainly improve your skills on a given subject, as indeed will committing to a lifetime learning process. But in any walk of life the benefits of having a great coach or mentor are proven time and time again.

In times of trouble sometimes what you most require is someone to listen and reassure you, someone you can trust. In your professional life, whether it's about decision making, or just for general advice, having someone you can trust and rely on to help you make that right decision is critical to future success.

Prime ministers and presidents, kings and queens and leaders from all walks of life surround themselves with advisors and key people to help them through the decision making process.

In the world of sport, raw talent is turned into world-class performance as a result of expert coaching and advice from individuals who understand what it takes to achieve the ultimate success.

In the 21st century there is an abundance of counsellors, life coaches and mentors who provide a service to those people looking to improve their own performance and their lifestyles in general.

Coaches and mentors are not employed to make the decisions for you, they simply offer their best advice. Ultimately you remain in control of the final decision. After all, it's your life and after receiving the advice you must take responsibility and control of your own destiny.

When searching for and selecting a mentor or coach you should consider the following:

⇨ Be selective. Don't appoint the first person you meet.

⇨ Decide what it is that you are looking for in a coach.

⇨ Consider what it is you expect the coach or mentor to do.

⇨ Make sure it's someone you both like and trust otherwise it simply will not work.

⇨ Make use of your contacts. Ask around and see if there is anyone out there who comes recommended. Use all available research to source the right person for you.

⇨ Don't be afraid to seek references about your coach's credentials. Ask for names of some of their clients who you could talk to prior to making your final decision.

⇨ Be prepared to communicate your targets and goals, before making an appointment. Ask the potential mentor or coach how they can help you achieve those goals.

⇨ Your mentor or coach has to be right for you and you only. The chemistry must be right. The coach must understand you as a person and your needs and aims. If this doesn't come across at the outset, at the very beginning of your initial meeting, then they probably won't be the right match for you.

⇨ Finally, don't jump in. Keep searching until you are absolutely certain you've found the right person.

Since the beginning of mankind every one of us needs and benefits from mentoring and sometimes leadership, in all areas be it religious, social, family, educational, governing, professional or business. The fact is that without people who we can trust and from whom we can seek advice, there is simply no support mechanism to fully develop the potential we have within.

What benefits can a coach or mentor offer you as an individual?

⇨ A good mentor inspires your development and helps you realise your dreams.

⇨ A good coach analyses your skills and technique and works with you to enhance your performance and achieve better results over a period of time.

⇨ Coaches and mentors act as sounding-board, allowing you to discuss your targets and goals in confidence with someone you can trust.

⇨ Are you doing the right thing? Are you making the right decisions? Are you heading in the right direction? Mentors and coaches can help you answer these questions.

⇨ The right coach or mentor has to be experienced in their field. You can tap into this experience to enhance your own development.

⇨ Coaches and mentors provide advice and information on tap – all available for your benefit.

⇨ Coaches and mentors accelerate your development as an individual.

⇨ Coaches and mentors can help you identify and seek out new opportunities.

⇨ If you have potential a good coach or mentor will help you fulfil it.

⇨ If you're successful, the coach is successful and vice versa. A good coach or mentor will always have your best interest at heart.

Things to do:

⇨ Find yourself a mentor or coach if you're serious about developing you.

⇨ Start looking today.

⇨ Ask contacts in your own business circles for references.

⇨ Search on the internet for the service and person you're looking for and then make sure you check out their references thoroughly.

⇨ Write down your expectations. What do you want from a coach or mentor? Create a specification for the person you're looking for.

⇨ Set yourself some targets and goals to discuss with your coach or mentor.

⇨ Decide how much you can afford. Can you afford not to invest in you?

⇨ Set yourself a deadline to find a coach or mentor.

⇨ Always seek references.

⇨ If you are serious you can always contact me! Laurence@laurencewinmill.com

If you want to be the best, if you want to realise your potential and fulfil your ambitions, then you deserve to invest in your future. The right coach or mentor will certainly accelerate the process and ultimately they could prove to be the difference between success and failure.

26.

Reward success

Reward success

Having spent so much of your time planning the next step, setting targets and goals, making a commitment to others and to yourself, you deserve the chance to celebrate and reward your success.

When you set yourself goals, these targets are structured and vary across different time-scales. There may be several different steps or stages that you need to undertake before you achieve the goal. It is therefore important to recognise your success and reward yourself accordingly as you achieve and make positive progress towards your desired results. This process of work and reward makes you feel good about your achievements and creates a desire which drives you on to the next target.

Too many people make the mistake of not taking time out to celebrate their achievements and recognise and reward their success. The risk here is that failure to recognise performance could have a negative impact on your motivation levels, and without that burning desire for success, your achievement levels will begin to wane.

It is important for your self-esteem to acknowledge all the things that you do well. Create a log or file and record all your successes – they are too precious to be forgotten.

People often spend too much time dwelling on past failures. Learn to accept them, then forget them and move on with optimism, celebrating each and every success as it occurs.

Your successes should be tied into your goals and should apply to all aspects of your life whether it's spiritual, personal, business, educational, family or social. By setting goals as we discussed earlier, you can measure and identify your successes very easily, which means you need never miss the opportunity to celebrate the successes you achieve.

Always celebrate success with those who have helped you achieve that goal. By doing so, everyone involved in the process will have an appreciation of the effort that has gone into it, and you will be acknowledging the part they had to play in the final result.

It is important to reward anyone who has helped you achieve your successes. Saying thank you makes them feel valued so let others really see that their effort has been appreciated and their personal contribution has had an important influence on the final result.

It is important to understand that anyone who has achieved anything of significance in life and enjoyed sustained success, will openly tell you that it was made possible by the support and advice from people they trust. Doing anything in isolation can be lonely, frustrating and could limit you in terms of the results you produce.

As human beings we all need help, support and guidance to achieve our desires and when you achieve the success you crave, make the effort to celebrate in style with all those who helped make it possible.

Things to do:

⇨ Be sure of your goals in all areas of your life and reward every success.

⇨ List your targets and goals carefully within structured time-scales and reward every achievement.

⇨ Reward others who help you achieve your goals.

⇨ Celebrate success with the people who are important to you.

⇨ Treat yourself every time you achieve a result. Go to the cinema or take your partner for dinner. Visit the theatre or enjoy a weekend break.

⇨ Set targets with your team members and reward them for their contribution in attaining your goals.

⇨ Always talk about your goals and targets with those close to you and with those who are contributing to them. They will understand the overall objective and will be delighted to feel part of the overall success.

⇨ Create a success file or log. You'll find this very handy when things are not going so well. It will remind you of your past successes and will help reassure you that, despite challenges, you are a successful person.

⇨ Remember that loss of form is only temporary in any walk of life, but style is permanent.

⇨ Stay positive, stay focused and you will be successful.

27.

Make the most of your time

Live each day as though it were the last

Make the most of your time

Live each day as though it were the last.

Enjoy your life. It will not last forever so live every moment as if it were your last. Do you get up each morning dreading what the day has in store? Do you spend Sunday evenings feeling depressed about the week ahead? Are you watching the clock at work, counting down the hours until the end of your shift?

Why are you wishing your life away? What would you do if you suddenly realised that tomorrow was your last day on this planet? I'm sure you would have a different outlook about how to spend the little time you had left.

Although we've talked about making plans, setting goals and working towards them, it's important that you also make sure your journey is a happy one.

If thinking about the week ahead is very depressing, take control of the situation and ask yourself what is causing you to be so unhappy. If you can't change the way you feel about your situation then you must take responsibility to change what it is in your life that is making you unhappy.

This applies equally to your business and your personal life. If you can't stand your job – change it! If you hate being with your partner and the relationship is making you miserable, then change your partner! Life is simply too short to be unhappy for long periods of time.

If you live in a wet climate, learn to accept the weather. You can't change the weather, so go out and feel the rain on your face and start enjoying the climate you live in. If you hate it to the point where it's making you miserable then consider moving to a part of the world where you will find the happiness you so desire.

Be positive about you, your life and what you're doing with your life. Seek contentment and be happy. Simply enjoy the moment.

I recently picked up the following story from a friend of mine. I don't know if it's true and I don't know who wrote it but I love every word of it:

CARPE DIEM!

An eighty-five-year-old man who learned that he had just a few days to live wrote the following piece:

"If I had my life to live over again, I'd try to make more mistakes next time. I wouldn't be so perfect. I would relax more. I'd limber up. I'd be sillier than I've been on this trip. In fact, I know very few things that I would take seriously. I'd be crazier. I'd be less hygienic.

I'd take more chances, I'd take more trips, I'd climb more mountains.

I'd swim more rivers; I'd go more places I've never been to.

I'd eat more ice cream and fewer beans.

I'd have more actual troubles and fewer imaginary ones!

You see, I was one of those people who lived prophylactically and sensibly hour after hour, day after day, year after year.

Oh, I've had my moments, and if I had it to do over again, I'd have more of those moments – moment by moment by moment.

I've been one of those people who never went anywhere without a thermometer, a hot water bottle, a gargle, a raincoat and a parachute.

If I had it to do all over again, I'd travel lighter next time.

If I had it to do all over again, I'd start out earlier in the spring and stay away later in the fall. I'd ride more merry-go-rounds,

I'd watch more sunrises; I'd play with more children,

If I had my life to live all over again.

But you see I don't."

I don't feel I can add much more to this subject which hasn't already been covered by these wonderful thoughts of this eighty-five-year-old man. So my advice to you is to take on board what he is saying: lighten up and enjoy being you. Don't be too serious about life, try to enjoy every single second you have at your disposal and live it to the full.

Things to do:

⇨ Listen to the advice given by eighty-five-year-old men and act upon it!

⇨ Don't wish away your life.

⇨ Spend time with people you love and people who make you laugh.

⇨ Learn to be at peace with nature. Love the rain, the hail, the snow, the wind and the sun.

⇨ Find hobbies and interests that give you pleasure.

⇨ Travel as much as you can.

⇨ Fulfil your potential. Do not become frustrated by failure. Never give up following your dreams.

⇨ Spend time with your family and loved ones and play with your children.

⇨ Make a habit of smiling as often as you can about every situation, every single day.

⇨ Seek a lifestyle that keeps you mentally and physically able so that you can live the life you choose.

⇨ Be happy.

28.

Travel

Travel

We live in a wonderful world of natural beauty: diverse climates, changing landscapes, huge oceans, rolling deserts, tropical jungles, snow-capped mountain terrain, white sandy beaches, barren hills and lush vegetation. Creatures large and small: plants, insects, predating beasts, beautiful birds that soar high in the sky and a huge variety of fish that populate the seas from the Arctic in the north to the Antarctic in the south.

There is so much to see and so little time in which to do it, so don't waste the opportunities that come your way. My advice to you is to travel and explore this planet whenever you can. Experience different cultures, meet new people and see the many wonders of the world.

You can begin at home. Get out and see what's on your own doorstep. No matter where you live there is always plenty to see and lots to explore. You'll find architecture, museums, galleries, theatres and art centres, some large, some small, close by wherever you live.

You'll find urban trails, country walks, beautiful beaches, magnificent cities and industrial heritage all within reach if you just make the effort to look. In the 21st century, travel for the majority is cheap and easy. If walking isn't possible you have a choice between bicycles, cars, trains, coaches, aeroplanes and ships, all providing a service to those who chose to travel.

You simply have to make the effort, plan the time and do it.

The youth of today certainly set the pace as they take advantage of the opportunities that my grandfather could only dream about. Very often students take a year out from their education and use that time to do exactly what I've been talking about. They visit specialist travel advisors and plan trips overseas that can last up to one year with the aid of a special travel visa. This allows them to travel between countries and continents, living cheaply but experiencing the wide variety of cultures that exist. Very often the stay will include a mixture of play and paid work in different countries to help finance the year away from home.

This is fine for the young but if your circumstances are different – you have a family, for example – you can still plan your vacations and holidays. These annual adventures will have a positive effect on your life because it becomes a real treat, something very different and exciting to look forward to.

Create a precedent for your kids: encourage them to travel and to broaden their outlook on life and the world we live in.

As far as we know, we have only one opportunity on this fantastic planet, so make the most of it while you're here. Live life to the full, explore and admire the treasures that exist on your doorstep as well as those further afield.

There is no doubt that a travelled person becomes a more confident and wiser person. You owe it to yourself and your children to travel. From the beginning of time, man has felt the need to explore: from the tribes of Israel, to the European discoverers, from the Pilgrim Fathers who established the great American colonies to Neil Armstrong and his first steps on the moon.

It is in the blood and the genes of every human being to travel, seek and explore. Go out and begin your exploring today.

Things to do:

⇨ Make a commitment to travel.

⇨ Create a travel plan. Decide where you want to go and what you want to see. Allocate times against the plan – break it down into months, quarters and years.

⇨ Visit areas of local interest that exist in your immediate locality. A lot of these amenities and sights of interest are free.

⇨ Visit a travel specialist and ask them to help you plan a trip of your choice.

⇨ Book a trip and pay a deposit – this forces you to make a commitment to travel.

⇨ Visit different continents – it's cheap and easy and you can be anywhere in the world within twenty-four hours.

⇨ Visit places of great natural beauty and admire the power of nature.

⇨ Take advantage of all the different transportation methods available to you. Sailing is very different from flying so experience both.

⇨ Watch travel programmes on television – they will inspire you with ideas about where to go and what to see.

⇨ If you can't find anyone to travel with, go alone. The experience will teach you a lot about yourself and it will force you to talk to people that you've never met before.

⇨ When you do travel, show respect for the environment, the countries and the cultures that you visit, and the people you meet.

⇨ When you return from your travels start planning the next trip.

29.

Accept responsibility

Accept responsibility

Stop blaming other people for your mistakes. Unless you have a gun pointed at your head or are in another adverse situation, you will always have a choice. You decide the course of action to take and therefore you must accept the outcome of your actions.

The sooner you stop blaming other people, the better you will feel about yourself and the way you live your life.

You had no say in being born into this world, but now that you're here, you have to get on with life and make the best of what you have.

Did you ever fail an exam in school or college? Whose fault was it that you failed? Yours of course! If you'd listened more in class, if you'd worked harder, revised more and asked more questions when you didn't understand, then I'm sure you would have passed! I know because it's happened to me, yet, at the time like others, I blamed everyone else rather than accept responsibility myself!

I blamed the teacher for his inadequacies. I blamed my parents for sending me to the school in the first place. I blamed the school for just being a school. I blamed my classmates for distracting me during lessons and I blamed the television for distracting me from doing my homework when I was at home.

Isn't it funny that not once did I consider blaming myself, until I realised that if I was to pass this particular examination I HAD TO TAKE RESPONSIBILTY AND CHANGE MY ATTITUDE AND BEHAVIOUR.

It was only when I did this that I eventually passed the exam. Everything we do in life is affected by our attitudes and behaviour. Change the attitude, change the behaviour – and get a different set of results.

Do you blame your manager at work for making the wrong decisions, for making your job even harder than it already is? What would happen if they changed the manager? How long would it be before you started to find fault in the new manager? Everything has a novelty value and when the novelty wears off, you start to find fault in whatever is left.

What could you do yourself to improve your attitude and performance at work? Instead of pointing the finger at someone else, take a look in the mirror. Are you absolutely certain that you're totally free of any blame? Try working with your manager and colleagues instead of working against them. Look for the good in others and be honest about your own inadequacies. You will start to feel more positive about yourself and your life in general by taking full responsibility for your actions and the decisions that you make.

What about your relationship and home life? Do you ever find yourself at loggerheads with your partner over something that might be of your own doing?

Why waste so much negative energy trying to win a stupid argument that only you care about? Couldn't you accept that a decision you made might have caused the problem? Surely the easiest way to get a resolution is to accept that it was your fault, deal with it, apologize if necessary and move on.

One hundred years from now you and I will be long gone so don't waste time defending indefensible nonsense that is too trivial to appear in any future history books. Accept responsibility, take control of your life and the decisions you make and be at peace with those around you and your inner self.

Things to do:

⇨ Be honest with yourself.

⇨ Be honest with others.

⇨ Learn to say sorry when you get things wrong.

⇨ Ask yourself: "Are you being reasonable and fair?" or is your behaviour negative and unnecessary?

⇨ You can't alter the past. Forgive, forget and move on. The forgiving and forgetting applies to forgiving yourself as well as others. Forgive yourself, learn from it and then move on.

⇨ Think carefully about decisions that could impact others. Is the risk of upsetting someone, a risk worth taking?

⇨ Encourage others, including those close to you, to take responsibility for their own actions.

⇨ Don't get too serious about life. Yes, you should take responsibility for your actions, but that's different from becoming a boring "Mr or Mrs Responsible" who has forgotten how to enjoy life.

⇨ Be aware that you are a role model in the eyes of others. Whether at work, at home or as a father there is always someone analysing your behaviour. Live life to the full, but don't let them down.

⇨ Be consistent in how you deal with accepting responsibility. You don't want to be regarded as having a "Jekyll and Hyde" character.

30.
Life

Life

Here we are at the last chapter of this book on living your life. I certainly don't have all the answers, indeed I don't know anyone who has but I genuinely hope that I've given you some helpful advice for making the most of your life, fulfilling your potential and finding a balance that keeps you at peace with yourself and those close to you.

I've dedicated this final chapter to some philosophical messages about life in general.

The first is a message by George Carlin an American comedian of the 1970's and 80's. As he was known for being a little foul-mouthed, it is fascinating that after the death of his wife and the 9/11 event, he would write so thoughtfully.

The second message is one I read recently which made me smile. I don't know the name of the author but as a child of the sixties it brought home to me some of the more crazy changes we are undergoing and the worrying over-protective nature of our society in the 21st century.

The third and final message is a famous poem written by Max Ehrmann, a poet and lawyer from Terre Haute, Indiana, who lived from 1872 to 1945.

Like the action points, ***"Things to do:"*** I have listed throughout, Ehrmann's poem, "Desiderata", provides a great inspiration to all those seeking a peaceful and well-balanced life. I believe it's one of the best lists of ***"Things to do"*** which has ever been published and I encourage you to read, digest and follow its advice.

Message Number 1 – A wonderful Message by George Carlin:

The paradox of our time in history is that we have taller buildings but shorter tempers, wider freeways, but narrower viewpoints. We spend more, but have less; we buy more, but enjoy less. We have bigger houses and smaller families, more conveniences, but less time. We have more degrees but less sense, more knowledge, but less judgment, more experts, yet more problems, more medicine, but less wellness.

We drink too much, smoke too much, spend too recklessly, laugh too little, drive too fast, get too angry, stay up too late, get up too tired, read too little, watch TV too much, and pray too seldom. We have multiplied our possessions, but reduced our values. We talk too much, love too seldom, and hate too often

We've learned how to make a living, but not a life. We've added years to life not life to years. We've been all the way to the moon and back, but have trouble crossing the street to meet a new neighbour. We conquered outer space but not inner space. We've done larger things, but not better things.

We've cleaned up the air, but polluted the soul. We've conquered the atom, but not our prejudice. We write more, but learn less. We plan more, but accomplish less. We've learned to rush, but not to wait. We build more computers to hold more information, to produce more copies than ever, but we communicate less and less.

These are the times of fast foods and slow digestion, big men and small character, steep profits and shallow relationships. These are the days of two incomes but more divorce, fancier houses, but broken homes. These are days of quick trips, disposable diapers, throwaway morality, one night stands, overweight bodies, and pills that do everything from cheer, to quiet, to kill. It is a time when there is much in the showroom window and nothing in the stockroom. A time when technology can bring this letter to you, and a time when you can choose either to share this insight, or to just hit delete.

Message Number 2 – "I can't believe we made it!" (Source unknown)

If you lived as a child in the Fifties, Sixties or Seventies then looking back – it's hard to believe that we have lived as long as we have.

As children, we would ride in cars with no seat belts or air bags. Our cots were covered with brightly coloured lead-based paint. We had no childproof lids on medicine bottles, doors and cupboards and when we rode our bikes we had no helmets. We drank water from the garden hose and not from a bottle. Horrors!

We would spend hours building go-carts out of scraps and then ride down the hill, only to find we had forgotten the brakes. After running into the bushes a few times we learned to solve the problem.

We would leave home in the morning and play all day as long as we were back when the streetlights came on. No one was able to reach us all day. No mobile phones. Unthinkable!

We got cut and broke bones and broke teeth and there were no lawsuits from these accidents. They were accidents! No one was to blame but us. Remember accidents?

We had fights and punched each other and got black and blue and learned to get over it. We ate cakes, bread and butter and drank cordial but we were never overweight. We were always outside playing. We shared one drink with four friends, from one bottle and no one died from this.

We did not have Play stations, iPads, video games or 65 channels on pay TV or even mobile handsets. We had friends! We went out and found them. We rode our bikes or walked to friend's homes and knocked on the door or rung the bell or just walked in and talked to them. Imagine such a thing! Without asking a parent! By ourselves! Out they're in the cold cruel world! Without a guardian – how did we do it?

We made up games with sticks and tennis balls and ate worms and although we were told it would happen, the worms didn't live inside us forever.

Football and netball had try-outs and not everyone made the team. Those who didn't had to learn to deal with disappointment.

Some students weren't as smart as others so they failed a grade and were held back to repeat the same grade.

Tests were not adjusted for any reason!

Our actions were our own. Consequences were expected. No one to hide behind! No speed humps! The idea of a parent bailing us out if we broke the law was unheard of. They actually sided with the law – imagine that!

This generation has produced some of the best risk-takers and problem solvers and inventors ever. The past 50 years has been an explosion of innovation and new ideas.

We had freedom, failure, success and responsibility and learned to deal with them all.

And you're one of them! Congratulations!

If you feel inclined – pass this on to others who have had the luck to grow up as kids before lawyers and government regulated our lives for our own good!

Message Number 3 – "Desiderata" written by Max Ehrmann in the 1920's.

Go placidly amid the noise and the haste, and remember what peace there may be in silence.

As far as possible, without surrender, be on good terms with all persons. Speak your truth quietly and clearly; and listen to others, even to the dull and the ignorant; they too have their story. Avoid loud and aggressive persons; they are vexatious to the spirit.

If you compare yourself with others, you may become vain or bitter, for always there will be greater and lesser persons than yourself. Enjoy your achievements as well as your plans. Keep interested in your own career, however humble; it is a real possession in the changing fortunes of time.

Exercise caution in your business affairs, for the world is full of trickery. But let this not blind you to what virtue there is; many persons strive for high ideals, and everywhere life is full of heroism. Be yourself. Especially do not feign affection. Neither be cynical about love, for in the face of all aridity and disenchantment, it is as perennial as the grass.

Take kindly the counsel of the years, gracefully surrendering the things of youth. Nurture strength of spirit to shield you in sudden misfortune. But do not distress yourself with dark imaginings. Many fears are born of fatigue and loneliness.

Beyond a wholesome discipline, be gentle with yourself. You are a child of the universe no less than the trees and the stars; you have a right to be here. And whether or not it is clear to you, no doubt the universe is unfolding as it should.

Therefore be at peace with God, whatever you conceive Him to be. And whatever your labours and aspirations, in the noisy confusion of life, keep peace in your soul.

With all its sham, drudgery, and broken dreams, it is still a beautiful world. Be cheerful. Strive to be happy.

This book took seven years to complete and along the way there was always a reason to re-edit and not publish. Well, there comes a time when everything must be concluded, so at last I've pressed the print button and should have done so much earlier!

I hope you've enjoyed the read, and that you've taken some inspiration from at least a few of the messages that this book provides.

Whatever your feelings, at the very least – go **live your life**...

Bibliography

Sources of 'Trivia Facts' and inspirations:

1. Page 7 & 12: http://www.at-bristol.org.uk/aboutus.html

   At-Bristol is a registered charity and one of the UK's leading science and discovery centres, where exploration and education go hand in hand with an unforgettable, fun day out.

2. Page 16: The Mexican Boatman:
   http://www.peterthomson.com/biography.php

   Peter Thomson is regarded as one of the UK's current leading strategists on business and personal growth. Starting in business in 1972 he built three successful companies – selling the last to a public company, after only five years trading, for £4.2M enabling him to retire at age 42.

   Since that time Peter has concentrated on sharing his proven methods for business and personal success via audio and video programmes, books, seminars and conference speeches. With over 100 audio and 100 video programmes written and recorded, he is Nightingale Conant's leading UK author.

3. Page 22: Attitude Quotes – W. Clement Stone

4. Page 38: Edison – Peter Thomson TGI Mondays:
   http://www.tgimondays.com

5. Page 43: Emmet Fox

   The author Emmet Fox makes a great point called "Tail Wags the Dog" and it's from his book "*Make Your Life Worthwhile*". In part it reads: "Truth is that your outer conditions – your environment – are the expression of your mentality, and nothing more. They are not cause; they are effect. They do not come first; they follow after...You do not have faith because things are going well. They are going well because you have faith. You are not depressed because trouble has come to you, but trouble has come because your realization of the Truth had first fallen off. Man is not limited by his environment. He creates his environment by his beliefs and feelings. To suppose otherwise is like thinking that the tail can wag the dog."

6. Page 45: A poem hangs on the wall in Mother Theresa's orphanage in India.

7. Page 53: Read 'Human Motivations' by **Abraham Harold Maslow**. Maslow (April 1, 1908 – June 8, 1970) was an American psychologist who was best known for creating Maslow's hierarchy of needs, a theory of self-actualization

8. Page 89: Armstrong Worldwide Industries: http://www.armstrong.com/

   The following is an extract taken from Armstrong's corporate history. It is an extremely strong example of the importance of values:

   Armstrong's founder, Thomas Morton Armstrong, turned the old business maxim Caveat emptor –"Let the buyer beware" – on its head and replaced it with five simple words, "Let The Buyer Have Faith".

9. Page 115: **Message Number 1 – A wonderful Message by George Carlin.**10) Page 118: **Message Number 3 – "Desiderata" written by Max Ehrmann in the 1920's.**

www.ingramcontent.com/pod-product-compliance
Lightning Source LLC
Chambersburg PA
CBHW060613200326
41521CB00007B/764